As a meditation teacher, I have found Marjorie's way of talking about inquiry to be refreshing. *Inquiring Deeply* is not about asking questions and getting answers. It teaches us how to grow a dialogue that leads to discoveries. And this book contains insightful and inspiring essays that will get you to think differently about the conversations you have. I hope all my meditation students read it.

— Jason Siff, Author of *Unlearning Meditation* and originator of Recollective Awareness Meditation.

This book of essays is a result of the author's own deep and self-challenging inquiries about how to find freedom *within* rather than freedom *from* problems. Interweaving and integrating the similarities and differences between dynamic/analytic therapies and Buddhist spiritual practices, these insightful essays provide rich material for deep reflection. They generously offer prompts for awareness practice and, ultimately, show us how to work with problems to cultivate creativity, wisdom and compassion. *Inquiring Deeply* is a remarkable and cutting-edge gift to readers, bringing the depth and width of working in mindful, relational, analytic, existential and spiritual work. What a joy!

– Eng-Kong Tan, MBBS, FRANZCP., *Founder President, Australian Association of Buddhist Counsellors & Psychotherapists, Adjunct Professor, Nan Tien Institute, Australia.*

Inquiring Deeply

Marjorie Schuman, Ph.D.

Inquiring Deeply

Problems as a Path to Awareness

Marjorie Schuman, Ph.D.

Inquiring Deeply
Press

Inquiring Deeply: Problems as a Path to Awareness

Print Edition ISBN 979-8-218-26771-1
Ebook Edition ISBN 979-8-218-26772-8

Cover Photo from Shutterstock

Cover design and formatting by Leo Baquero
leo_baquero@hotmail.com – layoutadaptationdesign.com

Table of Contents

Dedication

With gratitude to all of my partners in deep conversation.

The essays in this book were selected from INQUIRING DEEPLY
NEWSLETTERS published on the author's website,
www.drmarjorieschuman.com, between 2018 and 2023.

Section I

The Method of Inquiry

1

"Inquiring Deeply" Defined

Inquiry, the practice of looking deeply within, is a foundational practice in many contemplative traditions, including Buddhism. As a method of spiritual practice, inquiry seeks direct, experiential answers to basic questions about existence: Who am I? Where did I come from? Why am I here? What is the most important thing? The purpose of inquiry as a spiritual practice is to gain deeper insight and understanding into your own essential nature.

In addition to these kinds of lofty, existential questions, the method of inquiry is also suitable for exploring important personal and psychological questions, such as *What should I do? What do I want? Why am I unhappy? What am I doing wrong? How can I solve this problem or predicament?* To distinguish this second set of questions from the first, I coined the phrase "Inquiring Deeply", (defined and elaborated at length in my book by the same title).[1]

Inquiring Deeply can perhaps best be described as the **art and practice of asking oneself questions and then listening for your own answers**.

To inquire is to "live in" the question of something, simply staying as receptively alert as possible to whatever answers may emerge in the mind, body, and/or in events of life. **Inquiry is NOT an intellectual process, nor a process of trying to figure something out or make something happen. It is a process of ALLOWING wisdom to unfold.** The process is initiated by the conscious framing of a question, with the intention to listen deeply for what may be discovered.

Inquiry questions may be about anything troublesome, confusing or unresolved for you. They may be generated by something that preoccupies you, something that simply floats to the front of your awareness, or something that arises as you interact with others. Having framed a question, your task is simply to remain receptive to whatever answers may appear.

Deep inquiry has several different experiential dimensions. It begins with whatever comes to the surface in present-moment experience: sensations in the body, sights and sounds, thoughts, images, and emotions. It follows the slipstream of experiences and mind states as these change over time. Rather than focusing on "answers", inquiry is the process of staying open to whatever emerges, allowing the question to be a catalyst for a deeper awareness to develop.

I often liken this inquiry process to an extended conversation that takes place both within myself and in the external world simultaneously. It often seems as though life is alive and responsive to my inquiry; that answers are called forth by my intention to "answer" a particular question.

Each issue of INQUIRING DEEPLY NEWSLETTER presents the answers I have found in my own practice of inquiry about particular questions.

2

The Need To Know

"We don't know who discovered water,
but we're certain it wasn't a fish"

— John Culkin

Patterns of thinking are held in place, in part, by the need to know.

In the face of any negative experience—when we are anxious or threatened or in pain— we instinctively try to think our way out of the situation. For many people, this becomes a basic strategy for solving problems: "figure out" what to do. Over time, we become reliant on this effort to *know*. This strategy solidifies into an unconsciously held and deep belief that knowing is essential to safety (or at least the illusion of safety). We cling to knowing as a primary source of security. Knowing allows us to feel more in control.

Alongside this attachment to knowing, we can also observe the tendency to defend what we know (or what we believe we know). We can notice that we cling to what we believe, and we can observe how we attempt to prove to ourselves (and others) that our views are right. Clinging to beliefs reflects the fact that our opinions and views often come to be invested with a sense of self.

At a yet more fundamental level, we can see how we identify with the *faculty* of knowing: we *become* the knower, never noticing, much less questioning, the assumption that *who I am is the one who knows*. Indeed, the function of knowing is a basic aspect of the conscious mind, integrally involved in giving rise to the sense of self. So, whatever it is I take my *self* to be, the ability to know is at the core of it.

This kind of self-identity rests on several false assumptions. Self-as-knower is based on what we have come to know in our lives along with all of its associated beliefs and assumptions. It may readily become a closed circuit that limits our thinking, our relating, and our way of being in the world. When we inquire deeply about what we know, we can begin to see that what we think we know keeps us from seeing what we don't know, which is nearly everything.

When, in contrast, we are able to let go of needing to know and can relax into not having all the answers, we can begin to access a domain of deeper awareness that is based not in what we know but in the simple experience of being. Such open and authentic experience of the present moment allows the emergence of insight and creativity. As we learn to locate ourselves in the experience of not knowing, we can begin to transcend limiting identifications with the self as knower.

"Thinking we know costs us everything we don't know — which is nearly everything".

—Gregory Kramer [2]

3

Inquiring Deeply About
How We Change

Many — most — things that cause suffering are beyond our control. But even those circumstances where it appears we *do* have some choice may be stubbornly persistent, hard to manage, or intractable. Life has a momentum that tends to carry our problems forward into the future for reasons both seen and unseen. We suffer from what psychoanalysts called **"repetition compulsion"**: the tendency to repeat old patterns over and over again, reenacting painful events or putting ourselves in situations where the same dreaded outcomes are likely to happen again.

Sometimes we bear our struggles and miseries with an added sense of shame that we must have brought them upon ourselves as a result of our own unworthiness. Nonetheless, within us there is a potentiality for change. Freedom lies in the wise awareness of alternatives and of the ability to choose. How can we cultivate this freedom?

In order to come to terms with our problems, it is helpful to have someplace to "put them." Very broadly, we need to understand what we think needs to change, and probe the reasons why. Change is facilitated when we also have the following:

1) A good psychological frame/narrative view which is "user friendly" and in which we can relate to ourselves with affection and without harsh judgment.

2) A psychological "container": emotional support sufficient to allow us to relax with the situation, make space for what is happening, and breathe space into the problem. (These are different ways of saying that we have to find a way to accept what is happening; to stop struggling against it.)

3) A relational home: a context of human understanding within which the situation can be held and integrated. [3]

These dimensions of support allow us *feel into* the problem or difficulty. When we can be deeply present with what is happening, we can see the situation more clearly and discern what is wanted and needed; what is wise.

Problems entail any number of dysfunctional, ego-centered assumptions, but they also direct our attention to what we need to see. The pain associated with a problem can point to how we are unnecessarily limiting ourselves. The perspective that a problem has value can itself represent an important existential shift. We can begin to see that **problems and their solutions are two sides of a single coin.**

In the framework of deep self-inquiry, we can approach stubborn difficulties by "living in the question" of them. Somewhat analogous to the Zen idea of "koan", this means that we endeavor to sit with the question; be with it; and repeatedly ask the question as a means of inviting a transformational shift of view. This idea first came to me in the form of an epiphany in which I recognized that *the problem was the problem!* The very notion that there *was* a problem, I saw, tended to lead me down a rabbit hole of trying to figure out how to get out from under it. Not only was overthinking a problem not useful, the process of struggle was counterproductive, distracting attention away from the feelings at the core of the emotional difficulty. Getting stuck in trying to figure things out often becomes a problem in its own right.

So where do solutions come from? I love the following example offered by the Zen teacher Richard Baker:

> *I dreamt I was trying to solve a problem. A brown phone kept ringing in the background, distracting me. Finally, annoyed, I picked it up. The voice on the other end told me the answer to the problem.*

Although we seldom dream of the solution to our difficulties, in the mystery of unconscious process solutions simply arrive one way or another. It is as if answers are summoned by our intention to discover something. For me, the emergence of solutions engenders the feeling that life is alive and responsive to the questions I ask.

Short of waiting for illuminations and epiphanies, there are strategies and practices that we can engage to cultivate change:

- **Clarify your intention**. "Inquire deeply" within about what you are trying to change, and why. What result are you trying to produce? What are you trying to be, do, or have? Who are you trying to become?

Endeavor to see your intentions clearly.

- **Clarify the obstacles**. "Inquire deeply" about how you may be getting in your own way.

  In addition to *what* seems to be in the way, notice especially *how* you are being in the present moment; what attitude(s) you are carrying?; how you are inhabiting yourself?; what you are embodying?

- **Clarify what is at stake for you**. How would you be different if life no longer contained this problem or challenge? Who would you be if there were no problem to solve?

- **Ask yourself: "Are you willing to be changed by change?"** [4]

The ability to change rests upon our wise and compassionate awareness of the matrix of meaning in which we live and construct our personal experience. We need to cultivate the awareness and self-reflection that will make this possible.

4

Problems As Path

A central tenet of my book, INQUIRING DEEPLY [1], is that problems are a basic organizing principle in psychological life. Consider, for example, (as every reader can certainly notice) the fact that everyone has problems. In my view, problems have a role in our minds analogous to the role of pain in the body; problems call attention to what we most need to see.

Beyond the particular circumstances, we need to address the underlying view that having problems is itself a problem; as if life could be without problems or that having problems is an indication of deficiency or failure. Instead, problems can be seen as opportunities for growth.

The goal in a mindfulness-informed approach to problems is not to disappear problems (which of course is what most people hope will happen), but rather to deepen our awareness of them in lieu of overthinking them. The central premise is that solutions to problems emerge as a function of how clearly we can see where we are stuck. From this perspective, problems and solutions can be seen to be two sides of a single coin.

The path of problems follows along in the slipstream of our concern about a problem.

Problems are configurations or patterns in the mind which are organized around a nucleus of something too painful to be fully experienced. Such "nonexperienced experience" may be thought of as a logjam in the free flow of mental energy in the mind. Such patterns comprise the traumatic core of problems, which over time calcify or rigidify into a kind of "scar tissue" in our psychic structure, including character.

Bringing mindful and self-compassionate attention to the network of our associative connections gradually untangles the knots of pain and trauma in the psyche and helps to reveal aspects of our innate wisdom.

In INQUIRING DEEPLY [1], I delineate ten headings or "stepping stones" on the mindful path of problems: ten component factors in psychological change. The first tasks have to do with clearly identifying the problem and conceptualizing the leading edge or horizon of change which the problem represents. A related task involves deconstructing the experience of the problem; unpacking the problem into component elements of sensation, perception, thoughts, and feelings. Because problems crystallize around relational wounds, inquiring deeply about our relationships with others is primary. Together, this deep inquiry leads to the development of insight, clarity, and deep emotional understanding.

5

Practicing With Problems

What Is "Practicing With Problems?"

The idea of "practicing with problems" is adapted from "dharma practice", which means the ongoing application of Buddhadharma in one's everyday life experience. To "practice with", in a more generic sense, means simply to systematically engage in self-reflection about our subjective experience. "Practicing with problems" is a strategy for relating to our troublesome problems and circumstances by bringing deliberate, focused, and mindful attention to understanding what is going on with us.

Inquiry

As explained in previous issues of this Newsletter, **Inquiry** is the process of formulating a personal question and then listening within for whatever answers may emerge. To inquire is to "live in" the question of something, simply staying as receptively alert as possible to whatever answers may emerge in the mind, body, and/or in events of life. Inquiry is NOT an intellectual process, nor a process of trying to figure something out or make something happen. It is a process of ALLOWING wisdom to unfold.

I have found it interesting to reflect on the idea that **"?" is part of the basic grammar of the mind**. "?" launches a process of looking for answers. If you've ever had the experience of not being able to remember a word you're looking for (on the tip of your tongue, as it were), you know that it often happens that the forgotten word shows up in your mind minutes, hours, or even days later. This common experience demonstrates the nature of the unconscious circuitry of the mind. Simply by asking a question, we invite the unfolding of the answers.

Finding Relevant Questions

Frequently when I describe the process and purpose of Inquiry, people want to know "What should I ask?" That is a great first question! The common wisdom is: Start where you are.

It's important to understand that the CONTENT of what you ask (the Question) is only part of what's important about Inquiry. Equally important, or arguably more important, is the mindset we bring to Inquiry; receptivity to PROCESS.

In practicing with problems, inquiry questions morph, evolve, and deepen over time. The following example will convey the basic idea: I woke up in an off mood and wasn't immediately able to connect it with a dream or any other recent event. Curious about what was bothering me, I decided to make this question the object of focus in my morning meditation. I first turned my attention to what I was feeling and simply inquired *"What is this about?"* I soon recognized that this train of thought was connected to my apprehension regarding an upcoming social event. Although social anxiety is not uncommon for me, I pressed myself to look more deeply into the question *"What am I scared of?"* As I unpacked the various levels of answer to this question, I honed in on the experience of shame; I was averse to feeling shame. This led to the additional question: *"How I Am I Afraid I Will Be Seen?"* Over ensuing days this changed yet again into the question *"Who Am I Afraid I Am?"* and, eventually, the softer form *"Who Do I Aspire To Be?"*

Inquiry As The Unfolding of Wisdom

Fundamentally, I believe, what we actually seek when we engage Inquiry is to connect more deeply with our organic or intuitive intelligence. The template I rely upon is one I discovered in the process of recovering from physical injuries. While doing rehab at the gym, I learned that it was often more beneficial to mindfully feel my way through a workout than it was to execute a prescribed sequence of exercises. I discovered that the best workouts were those in which I was able (at least on some occasions) to surrender agency to the wisdom of my body, allowing my body to choose what movement or exercise needed to be done next. With careful embodied attention, my body seemed able to hone in on what was needed for its healing. By bringing awareness to the body in this way, somatic intelligence was able to reveal itself. The frame in such "somatic inquiry" is that whatever arises (including pain) is an expression of the organic intelligence of the body.

So, too, with the psychological process of Inquiry. An inquiry question serves as a container for our experience of problems and difficulties, framing an underlying intention to grow *with* and *from* awareness of our emotional life. When we Inquire, we repeatedly **look deeply into problems in a way that breathes space into them and allows their hidden meanings to emerge**. Inquiry is an intuitive process in which we *feel* our way forward through our challenges and difficulties, surrendering as best we are able to whatever arises in our experience.

Allowing Your Inquiry Practice To Find *You*

People often ask what Inquiry I recommend for them, or what tools or techniques they need to practice in order to solve their problems. In my response, what I generally try to illuminate is the underlying set of assumptions hidden within that question. What does the person feel so urgent about getting, doing, or having? (And: "What is at stake?") Are they being driven by aversion to current experience?

More important than what we *do* is how we are *relating* to ourselves. **When we prioritize the urgency of relief over the slowness of being present with what is, it is very easy to overlook the intuitive wisdom that is seeking to emerge.**

Through the intention to "practice with" our difficult and painful experiences, we can begin to embrace the radical possibility that our symptoms and problems are actually appropriate responses to some underlying sense of loss of meaning, purpose, and connection in our world of lived experience. Things begin to shift when we start to recognize that painful emotional states have their own intelligence, often to help us recognize what it is that we do not want to feel. The work given us to do is then to re-own, re-embody, and work through our disowned experience.

The art of Inquiry, of life-as-practice, is a practice unto itself.

6

Intention:
The Leading Edge of Change

"If you look hard enough for something,
eventually it will appear"

—Ashleigh Brilliant

Dynamic psychotherapies tend to emphasize the causal role of the past in the present, with little emphasis on the shaping impact of awareness going forward. It has been left to "new age" spiritual psychologies to fill in that vacuum with various forms of "thinking from the end": The fundamental idea that consciousness manifests that which it focuses on. Visualization, affirmation, positive thinking, and prayer, for example, are said to "create" whatever outcome is desired.

We can use the metaphor of pushing and pulling to explore these ideas of cause and effect. If we think of the past as a push and visualization as a pull, push and pull come together in the present moment by influencing how we interpret and respond to events in an ongoing fashion. In the act of bringing new awareness to the present moment, the next moment is already changed because of the alteration in view. In this way, insight about how something was brought about may become the beginning of what comes next. In metaphysical terms, *energy follows thought.*

Without resorting to metaphysics, the concept of *intention* in Buddhist psychology elegantly illuminates the complexity of this process. Intentions are an important dimension of thought because what we intend directs our energy and attention. Intentions frame our interpretations and determine how we hold things in mind. When we form a conscious intention, this then becomes an integral part of what unfolds next. **Attention and intention light up experience and support living from the inside out.**

Simple examples abound. If you are looking for someone to marry, everyone will be evaluated as a prospective mate. If you are angry and have the energy of ill will, you will find someone to fight with. If you expect good things to happen, the quality of your attention will itself amplify the possibilities of something good.

Because intentions are what "incline the mind" in one direction or another, it behooves us to be conscious of what these intentions are. Having clear intentions is a soft form of "thinking from the end." When our purpose is clear and coherent, we are on course toward a particular outcome. Moreover, intentions keep us centered in the moment by keeping our attention focused on what is important, and that helps us stay optimally responsive to what is unfolding.

Clear seeing and clear intention segue into strategies for action. Once we are clear about what the desired outcome *is*, we are poised to take whatever action is appropriate and indicated. (And conversely, our failure to see or understand important aspects of the current situation keeps us blind to important possibilities). Intention leads to constructive action in the spontaneous unfolding of the journey forward. It remains only to commit to what we most deeply value and stay on the path defined by putting one foot in front of the other.

By acknowledging the importance of intention, deep inquiry invites change. As the psychoanalyst Alan Wheelis put it, "something lies behind us, something goes before us, consciousness lies between."[5] This blueprint for change is expressed in the following aphorism:

> *First comes understanding, without which action*
> *is blind. Then comes action, without which*
> *understanding is ineffective. Finally, understanding*
> *and action become one.*

7

The Unfolding of Wisdom:
Going With The Flow

Wisdom is inherent within us, but it takes a concerted effort to learn how to listen deeply for the messages that life is "speaking." By following the thread of inner truth which is available in whatever we experience, we connect more and more deeply both with what is so and with who we are.

Wisdom is not abstract. It reveals itself in insights, both large and small, as well as in the answers we discover for our deep questions and in the resolutions we find for our most vexing problems. **Wisdom is a path**.

Wisdom is also a practice. By bringing alert receptivity to what we experience moment by moment, we increasingly discover whatever we need to see in what is going on; the meanings implicit in what is happening. In this way, we can endeavor to *receive* life: to open to life instead of struggling against it.

In cultivating wisdom, we attune ourselves to the simple truth of experience, including emotional experience. Wisdom unfolds naturally as we inquire about what is happening, and why; our deepening wisdom expresses itself in our ability to be increasingly present with ourselves and others.

Finally, **wisdom is a process**. In inquiry practice, we attune ourselves to finding the dynamic intelligence in the flow of awareness. To "go with the flow" of life as an unfolding wisdom *process* means to align ourselves with what is happening. Literally, we aspire to *be like water* — to flow in and around the events of life. Going with the flow is a kind of letting go in which we allow life to carry us downstream; surrendering to the currents of our life energy, whatever they may be, we heed the intelligence of our body, heart, and mind. In other words, we allow ourselves to evolve.

Ultimately wisdom reveals itself in a felt sense of the existential coherence in life, inclusive of all of its thematic complexities. In the words of the Gestalt therapist Barry Stevens, we learn not to push the river; it flows by itself. [6]

Section II:

Some Reflections on Thinking, Feeling, and Self

8

Inquiring Deeply About Self-Reflection

Self-reflection may be broadly defined as the process of examining our own experience in order to become aware of our thoughts and feelings. The word "reflection" itself evokes the idea of the mind as a mirror. We may become aware of many different kinds of images in the mirror of the mind: what we see and hear, what we feel, what we think. And, we also have the capacity to turn our attention back to the surface of the mirror itself.

We can distinguish among several different levels or degrees of self-reflection. In the most basic sense, self-reflection refers to the process of looking inward and deliberately examining one's thoughts, feelings, and actions. Self-reflection is a conscious activity, a form of self-analysis which allows us to gain insight into ourselves. In inquiry, self-reflection allows us to engage with basic questions such as *"Who Am I?"* or *"What Is My Heart's Desire?"*

The inborn cognitive capacity which underlies self-reflection is called **self-reflexive awareness**. Self-reflexive awareness is a function of feedback loops in the human brain/mind which operate without deliberate introspection. For example, self-reflexive awareness operates in the background of ongoing sensory, motor, and cognitive activities as a component of the experience of being conscious. At other times, it may move into the foreground of our attention, amplified through intentional focus (as in meditation) or by virtue of emotional reactions (e.g. social anxiety; embarrassment) or interpersonal events.

Although self-reflexivity is an inborn capacity, the ability to self-reflect expands and deepens along with other aspects of psychological development. It is organized in relation to our understanding of our own minds as well as the minds of others. Moreover, because some aspects of ourselves are essentially invisible except in the mirror of another, **our capacity to know ourselves is a function of our connection with others**.

Regardless, we can never become aware of ourselves from outside of our experience, only from within. So self-reflection is always both subjective and objective; it weaves together mind and body, thoughts and emotion, as it integrates both the observational and experiential dimensions of awareness.

Interpersonal experience is an important domain for the

development of self-reflection. Conflicts between ourselves and others call our attention to possible discrepancies between how we see ourselves and how we are seen. Such disruptions invite us to de-center from our own point of view and consider the impact we may be having on others. They also galvanize our attention to what would otherwise remain unseen in ourselves.

For all of us, psychological defenses in the mind are engaged in order to obscure vulnerable aspects of ourselves. We may deny or disavow realities which are painful, attribute qualities of ourselves to others, or find other ways to avoid knowing the truth about our feelings. **What we are blind to in ourselves is the limiting boundary of our freedom**.

Self-reflection is arguably *the* central integrative element in psychotherapeutic exploration and psychological growth. Reflecting on our experience and behavior either by ourselves, or in conversation with others (including psychotherapists), can help us to become aware of how we are relating to our experience. In seeing more clearly what we are doing, how we are feeling, and the way that we react to things, we create a greater capacity for choice. In this way, self-reflective awareness may be likened to a "clutch" which allows the mind to shift gears so that new points of view can emerge.

Self-reflection is an evolving dimension of our subjectivity which can be intentionally cultivated in practices such as meditation. Mindfulness meditation amplifies self-reflection through the intention to notice what one is aware of from moment to moment and through the ability to shift awareness from the content of experience to the context of background awareness which surrounds and contains it. This enhances the clarity of what is seen in the mirror of self-reflection and creates greater access to somatic, psychological, and relational layers of the mind.

Last but by no means least, with the cultivation of mindful attention we can become aware of awareness itself. This dimension of self-reflective awareness is the heart of many paths of meditation and spiritual practice. Its goal is to enable the practitioner to see more and more deeply into the body/heart/mind and into the nature of self, and ultimately, to experience transcendent states of consciousness. The practice of awareness of awareness can open the mind to directly experience connection with a higher power, whether that is understood as "True Self", a personal deity, the universe, or as universal consciousness.

It has been said that "Mindfulness is the state of mind in which you realize that you are more than your state of mind." The ultimate nature of transcendent awareness — awareness which lies beyond the mind — is beyond the scope of this Newsletter. The interested reader may enjoy reading the in-depth overview of awareness of awareness I wrote in the chapter entitled "Subjectivity and the Self" in my book, INQUIRING DEEPLY.[1]

9

To Think Or Not To Think:
That Is Not The Question

As is often said, the mind makes thoughts like water makes waves. So to think or not to think is not the question! The more appropriate question is how we relate to the process of thinking.

In my view, thinking in meditation is not merely the unwanted source of ruminative distraction it is often painted to be. To the contrary, there is transformative opportunity in paying attention to the content of the conversations that take place within our minds during meditation. The word "conversation" is useful in this context because it highlights the fact that **thinking itself is a relational process.** By paying close attention to inner dialogue, we can discover a great deal about our different "voices" or part-selves and can gain insight into the way we relate to ourselves.

Inner conversation is revealing. We may notice replays of actual conversations we have had with others, showing us what remains unfinished or where we have gotten emotionally snagged. Our minds may host soliloquies or arguments, even fantasize entire interactions with others. Inner conversation, like our communication with others, has many layers, interwoven with emotions and the bodily sense of our symbolized experience.

The themes represented in our mental narratives say a lot about how we "show up" in our interpersonal lives. We have an opportunity to get in touch with the stories we tell ourselves (consciously or unconsciously) about self and other. Our inner dialogues reveal our interpersonal assumptions, the interpretations and projections we tend to superimpose on others when we talk with them.

One important and often neglected dimension of the thinking mind in meditation is awareness of the mind's relationship to itself. We can begin by noticing the judgments and thoughts that we have about thinking. There is often a bias to view thinking as a kind of stepchild in the inner family. We may implicitly feel shame about the amount of mental bandwidth devoted to "story-teller mind."

Apart from the content of our mental narratives, there are also subtle aspects of our inner conversation that can be revealing. Do we feel ourselves to be Speaker? Listener? Neither? Both? Do we create sufficient space around what we say to ourselves to feel into the meaning of our inner conversation? Do we feel pushed around by our minds, driven crazy by our thinking? Do we rely on a kind of "thought police" to stifle our inner voices rather than to kindly investigate them? **To the extent that we view our job in meditation as managing and controlling the thinking mind, we**

may unwittingly enact a power struggle which is a form of self-violence.

It is ultimately the climate of our relationship with ourselves that allows transformative change to come into being. Any thought which we feel we must *not* think often represents a part of ourselves which has felt rejected, disappointed, frightened, ashamed, or otherwise hurt. Alternatively, when we make space in the mind for the process of thinking— when we can be present with thoughts and bring self-acceptance, compassion, and wisdom to investigating them— that creates the possibility for deep healing.

10

Wise Understanding of Emotion

One of the salient qualities of inner peace is **equanimity**, defined as the ability to maintain mental and emotional balance in the midst of whatever is happening. For human beings, emotional turbulence is a major source of challenge. Emotional balance, like walking a tightrope, requires both skill and practice. It rests on a foundation of a wise and compassionate understanding of emotional life.

I find it useful to engage awareness practice to amplify emotional experience around these issues. Deep inquiry — "Inquiring Deeply"— investigates emotional reactivity as a means of deepening understanding of emotional life. Both personally and professionally,

I find this method to be a powerful catalyst for emotional growth. The basic principles are simple:

- Make explicit your intentions, aspirations, and goals in regard to your emotional life. The main intention is *to be with* the experience of being upset. Other possible examples: to learn to sustain your experience of being centered (physical balance is a great analogue of this skill); to deepen your understanding of some particular emotional state — (e.g., the experience of being disappointed.)

- The most basic observation is *"being emotionally upset is like this."*[7] Then, inquire deeply about what you are feeling; what it is connected to; what is beneath *that*.

- Bring mindful awareness to the somatic experience of emotional activation and have the intention to relax into the experience. Emotion lives in the body. We process experience through the very act of bringing conscious awareness to it.

- Notice how you are relating to the experience of being upset. The goal is to not hold onto experience, push it away, or escape from it, but rather to simply be with, open to, and receive it.

- The primary goal in relating to emotional experience is for feelings to be felt more completely so that release and letting go can happen. Mindful awareness of emotional experience is key, but at the same time, it should be understood that letting go is not something that happens all at once. It occurs in stages through a process called "working through."

- It may not be skillful to just name emotions if in so doing you relate to your emotions like symptoms of a disease you are trying to cure or a problem you are trying to get rid of. The frame in which you hold emotional experience is important!

- Emotional reactivity is grounded in our interpersonal (relational) matrix of connection. It is not possible to deeply understand Self without also understanding Other. Psychological understanding of the dynamics between us is also very helpful.

- "Inquiring Deeply" about your emotional experience means to consciously engage your experience (on and off the cushion) with the attitude of delving into it, feeling whatever it is more fully, and inviting it to reveal itself. More than simply mindfulness of the moment, deep inquiry explores the meanings and messages conveyed in your emotional experience.

Ultimately, emotional equanimity is about "going with the flow" of experience. It rests on the broad foundation of our ways of being; what we may call our "life balance." Thus, at the psychophysiological level, for example, equanimity reflects our capacity to relax and rest; the balance between being active and being receptive. At the interpersonal level, it rests on the balance between being with others and being alone, plus our ability to be in harmony with others. And finally, at an existential level, equanimity is related to our energetic state. This includes the way we animate ourselves, our pace of life, and our capacity to be centered and present with What Is.

Practice finding mental and emotional balance in the midst of whatever is happening — perhaps especially when things are other than we wish them to be. This maximizes our ability to find the wisdom and compassion that is available in every moment.

11

On The Importance of
Being Understood

I had an upset this morning that crystallized something —or many somethings— for me. The upset centered around my feeling not understood by someone. "Not feeling understood" is in the same genre as *misunderstood*, but it is not quite the same. Discerning this distinction led me to recognize the many different flavors of meaning I attach to "being understood" (and "understanding"). Understanding is a spectrum of experience, not one single "thing." One size does not fit all.

As a psychologist and psychoanalyst, I have devoted my life to understanding others. In my effort to meet emotional experience

—both my own and that of others— in the best way I possibly can, I have given a lot of thought to the nature of emotional understanding. **Deep emotional understanding is direct comprehension grounded in intuition and empathy.** It is informed by concept and theory, but it is not only, nor primarily, conceptual.

Beyond extensive clinical study and experience, I have also spent years inquiring deeply about how deep emotional understanding lives in my own experience. I offer the following ideas for your reflection:

- **The psychological need to be understood is universal and basic to who we are as human beings.** "Understanding" has an important psychosocial function and is one of the basic moves in the dance of social communication and conversation.

- **Understanding is a basic element of intimate connection and is what allows us to feel emotionally safe.** To the extent that we feel accurately and empathically understood, we can trust and feel close to another.

- **Feeling understood is an important part of what makes it possible to learn to modulate our emotional states.** When we feel emotionally distressed, what we most need/want is to express our feelings and have them deeply received by an empathic Other. To feel well-met by a trusted other is a soothing balm for painful feelings.

  It is in safe connection with a trusted other that we are best able to relax and let go. This is what can release us from the clutches of painful feelings.

- **Conversely, lack of empathic understanding can be traumatic.** This can easily occur when the need for understanding is urgent. Lack of attuned understanding on the part of a needed Other can re-trigger old developmental wounds.

- **It is in the matrix of understanding between ourselves and others, especially in infancy and childhood, that we acquire basic learning about emotions and develop ways to cope with our feelings.** Our experience with intimate others, especially in infancy and early childhood, is the template for our emotional personalities.

- **It is in relationship with others that we learn how the human mind works.** Through our interactions with others, we come to understand mental states and the emotional dynamics involved in them. This understanding is the key to skillfully navigating the interpersonal domain.

Being upset signals the presence of something not yet seen, understood, and/or accepted. For this reason, there is great value in turning towards the upset and feeling our way toward deeper understanding. In order to move on, you must understand why you felt what you did and why you no longer need to feel it. It is useful to inquire deeply by asking ourselves questions (often implicit) such as:

- What am I feeling, and what triggered it?

- What wants/needs my attention?

- What am I clinging to?

- What am I avoiding?

- What do I not want to feel?

For me, deep emotional understanding is a basic relational aspiration. The essential ingredient is, I think, the intention to listen deeply to others, what they say verbally as well as nonverbally; both what they say and what they do not. I endeavor to perceive accurately and empathically what the other feels and to express what I have understood so that the other may feel deeply heard, seen, and received. That said, I do not mean to suggest here that every interpersonal interaction needs to be unpacked or analyzed. Deep listening is an art as well as a skill.

Last but not least, *what* we understand and *how we engage* with the *process* of understanding are integrally related. What we come to understand about another is not a fixed psychological reality but a dynamically changing function of the emotional interchange that unfolds between us. Our understanding will tend to reflect our ability to be present and open and will influence the feelings we have about the other. It will develop in relation to our empathy and curiosity, shaped by the questions we ask as well as what we learn from each subsequent experience. Through this process, wisdom and compassion can unfold at the leading edge of our understanding.

> *"We don't see things as they are,*
> *we see them as we are"*
>
> — Anais Nin

12

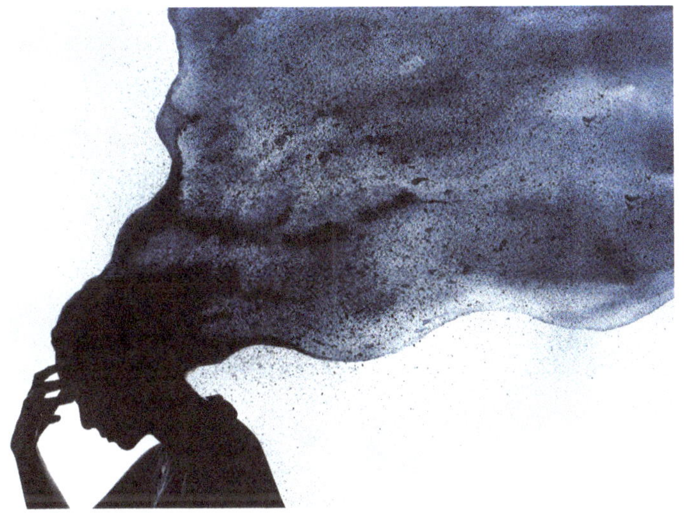

Inquiring Deeply About
Core Negative Beliefs

Core negative beliefs refer in a general way to judgmental and potentially harmful beliefs people hold about themselves. In this essay, I also opt to use the slightly different phrase *core negativity*, including both core negative beliefs and the negative mental states with which they are associated. A simple, experience-near definition of core negativity is the deep angst that there is something fundamentally wrong with us.

There is famous lore surrounding the Dalai Lama's response when asked about "self-hatred." Before he could answer, His Holiness had to confer at length with his translator. Although core negativity is fairly normative in the West, apparently it is sufficiently unusual among Tibetans that the translation of "self-hatred" is not straightforward. Be that as it may, in our culture aversion towards oneself is implicated in many common psychological afflictions, especially problematic anger, depression, anxiety, and shame.

In this Newsletter, I will first give what I hope is a lucid summary of the nature of core negativity and the negative beliefs we harbor about ourselves. Then, I will talk about a wise frame for self-reflective and meditative inquiry about them and how inquiry can be of benefit in working with them. It is my hope that this discussion will inspire readers to "inquire deeply" into their own core negativity.

What Is Core Negativity, and Where Does It Come From?

Most of us are aware of one or more areas in life where we harbor negative self-esteem, self-recrimination, or self-blame. We may be prone to states of negative mood, emotional "bad weather", and negative thought storms. Self-critical thoughts associated with core negative beliefs are usually not far from the surface, awaiting triggering by something someone says or does (or something that we say or do!). That said, our core negativity often tends to be apprehended in a somewhat vague way, because it lives partially submerged in the ocean of unconsciousness from which our psychological life emerges.

Core negativity is constellated around early relational wounds and becomes known to us primarily in states of emotional pain. It is rooted in painful relational events from the past: composite memories of how we were treated, what we felt at the time, and what we were explicitly told about ourselves when we were young and vulnerable. We are programmed with core negative beliefs in the process of our early experiences with family and significant others.

A prototypical memory might be something like this: We did something that made someone (usually a parent) mad, exasperated, or disgusted. "You're so stupid! Can't you do anything right?" Or, "You ruin everything! What's wrong with you!" The words hurt, but the emotional impact of the experience was even worse. We may have felt hated, unsafe. (We may have *been* hated and unsafe!) We took the angry, attacking judgments as true and internalized them as beliefs about what is wrong with us.

While generally it will be obvious to someone when they are in the thrall of core negativity, and while it is usually not difficult to identify what happened externally to trigger the distress, the internal roots of the emotional turbulence may not be so clear. The best practice opportunity for investigating core negativity is when something deeply upsetting comes along: a conflict with someone, a rejection or rebuff, a disappointment, insult, or invalidation. This situation affords an up-close and personal look at the elements of core negativity.

One of the biggest challenges in investigating core negativity is the tendency to locate the "problem" in the other person. For example, we may project undesirable attributes onto others, hiding what we are afraid to see in ourselves behind a curtain of externally-directed blame. When your spouse gets angry with you, for example, it's natural to focus on your perceptions and judgments about *them*, when what really needs your attention is what is going on inside of *you*. What experience does your spouse's anger trigger in *you* that you find overwhelming? What are you having trouble being with?

In the deep layers of the psyche, experience is "primary process": a mélange of archaic, primitively organized perceptions, feelings, and images. The differentiation between what is Self and what is Other is not a given; it has to be *learned*. (This topic is addressed at length in two Newsletters in Section III of this book which have the word "Entanglement" in their titles.) In any event, in order to work with negative beliefs which cause emotional distress, it is necessary that we first be able to own the attributions that belong to us.

Inquiring Deeply About Core Negativity

The frame for inquiry about core negativity is multi-layered, inclusive both of the psychological basis of core negativity and of the Buddhist view of what causes suffering.

"What Is This?"

Typically, inquiry begins with the simple intention to **investigate an experience of emotional pain**. The basic goal is to be able to **clearly discern what we feeling**: both what emotions have been activated and the negative thought patterns that are present. This inquiry has several components:

1) Locating where the emotion (or distress) is felt to be located in the body (although this may not always be clear). And/or,

2) Settling into the body while "listening in on" what the mind has to say about what is going on and the meaning we are giving it.

   As previously noted, when we have gotten upset in an interaction with someone else, it can be difficult to see clearly who is doing what to whom.

"What story am I believing now?" and: *"Is it really true?"*

Quite often emotional pain has to do with our ideas and beliefs about what is "wrong" with us. We have been told or have otherwise come to conclusions about the ways that we are deficient or inadequate. It can be useful to see the origin of these ideas in our earlier life experience. (**"Where did that story come from?"** and/or **"Where did I get that idea?"** and/or **"Who told me that?"**) And, it is important to reflect on the evidence upon which our negative views are based.

"Who am I afraid I am?" and/or "Who do I think I need to be?"

At a deeper level, inquiry about core negativity often becomes an inquiry about *self*. We need to see who we are afraid we are; or, how we are afraid we will be seen by others.

Moreover, on the flip side of the core negative—what we think is wrong with us— is its inverse: who we think we are supposed to be (or are supposed to become).

Psychotherapy and Core Negativity

Although psychotherapy can be very useful in working with core negativity, several common pitfalls are worth mentioning:

First, people often engage psychotherapeutic work with an expectation that core negative beliefs can be made to go away. Because core negativity is embedded in deep layers of the psyche which are pre-verbal or unconscious may, they are difficult to eradicate. A more realistic goal is to **develop a more nuanced awareness of core negativity and how it functions within us.**

Second, for the same reasons, the effort to actively counter negative beliefs with more rational positive alternatives — positive thinking, positive self-talk, or other self-affirmative assertions— is quite limited in its effectiveness. Because core negativity is rooted in regions of the psyche that are fundamentally emotional, relational, and non-verbal, cognitive "corrections" can only go so far in addressing it. **Core negativity needs to be experienced, not objectified**.

Third, because core negative beliefs reflect emotional wounding sustained in our primary relationships in early life, positive relational experiences are the best way to counteract them. **Relational wounds are best healed in relationship**.

And fourth, trying too hard to uproot negative beliefs is counterproductive. This is especially likely to happen among those who tend to be perfectionistic or have obsessive traits (quite common among those who struggle the most with core negativity). As the saying goes, **what we resist, persists**. The effort to overcome negative thinking can have the paradoxical effect of making negative beliefs seem more rather than less real.

Inquiry about core negativity is without these drawbacks. It enables us to discern what is cloudy, confused, or mistaken in our point of view about ourselves. Perhaps it is important to add that inquiry as a meditative practice does NOT mean running after thoughts, obsessing, or spinning out in thoughts about why. Instead, we *feel our way into* the experience of core negativity, and we endeavor to hold those parts of ourselves with kindness.

One underlying premise in deep inquiry that I have found to be very useful is beautifully stated in the following lines from psychiatrist Theodore Isaac Rubin: *"The problem is not that there are problems. The problem is expecting otherwise and thinking that having problems is a problem."*[8] Core negativity is part of our nature. The less we "problematize" it, the less we will suffer.

Core Negativity, Dharma Practice, And Deep Inquiry

It seems ironic that whereas every spiritual path tells us that what we seek is inside us, core negativity seems to proclaim the opposite: that we are fundamentally insufficient, unworthy, bad, or wrong. Therein lies the rub! In any event, spiritual "solutions" to core negativity seem to boil down to the following propositions:

- Negative beliefs are only thoughts, not actually "real", and, as such, are to be let go of.

  And/or

- The problem is simply that we are identified with the ego "I", the voice in our head that disparages us, worries, doubts, suffers, and fears losing control. If we do not believe those voices, we are told —if we do not reify ego—then the problem disappears.

In other words, **the "solution" to the "problem" of core negativity lies beyond belief**. Though simple in theory, for many different reasons this is much more easily said than done.

Inquiry allows us to see that believing is only one way to relate to something that may or may not be true. Once we wrap a belief in a question mark, we have already begun to undermine the very credulity upon which its existence depends. **There is power in holding open the question of what is true. It loosens the hold of belief on our experience.**

Inquiry can reveal our tendency to respond to core negative beliefs by closing down, blocking opportunities for growth that might otherwise be present. Conversely, when we are willing to look more openly, deeply, and compassionately at what we don't like about ourselves, we open new avenues for authentic self-acceptance and self-expression.

My experiences with deep inquiry have re-affirmed for me again and again that inquiry has a mind of its own. When we follow along in the slipstream of our curiosity, interest, and experience, our awareness of core negativity leads us naturally to a deepening of our wisdom and compassion.

13

Inquiring Deeply About Praise

The German novelist Thomas Mann apparently experienced quite a bit of anxiety about how his work would be received. He quipped that he suffered from a "P vitamin deficiency": chronic hunger for praise.

I resonate with the idea of vitamin P and the implied meaning that approval fills deep needs and is an essential psychological nutrient. It is quite evident that the need for approval is a driving force in human behavior, as well as being a basic regulator of self-esteem. We are **motivated to be seen** in a myriad of different forms. Praise and approval— as well as the close cousins mirroring, recognition, validation, and positive evaluation— are all very high in Vitamin P! Praise is an upper; and, on the other side of the coin, the failure to receive praise which is wanted, needed, or expected is emotionally upsetting.

So, what is this about? When we look into how the need for praise shows up in our experience, we confirm what Heinz Kohut postulated in psychoanalytic Self Psychology: **recognition and approval are self-delineating and life-affirming**. We seek validation for who we take ourselves to be, and in order to feel a vital connection to our core experience of self. In Buddhist psychology, the primal motivation is the hunger to Be, to exist.

When we do not get sufficient Vitamin P from important relational others—when we fail to be affirmed as valuable, special, worthwhile, and/or lovable— our incapacity to sustain a coherent sense of ourselves shows up as emotional turbulence. While each person's experience is somewhat idiosyncratic, the general tenor is usually anxiety, depression, or similar. What I find descriptive of my own experience is a sense of <u>deflation</u>: negative mood and self-critical ideation. The general idea of *contraction* seems to capture it.

The hunger to be seen is a primal relational desire: the **need to exist in the eyes of the other**. This deep relational need stems from the fact that humans need other humans to survive. To be abandoned as a helpless baby means certain death. Psychological survival, too, depends on being seen. This reality was dramatized in the classic novel of the 1980's, "Clan Of The Cave Bear,"[9] in which a homosapien woman was psychologically exiled for nonconformity to the tribal rules of her Neanderthal brethren. No one was to make eye contact with her. This was a brutal form of punishment.

Self is brought into being in relationship. The prototypical moment is the one that occurs in the first moments after birth, when the new baby looks into the eyes of a mother who is looking back. As

Kohut put it, the self at birth is a *virtual self*, a self which develops in the process of being seen and responded to by (m)other. This is true in earliest psychological life and remains so throughout the life span. **What is not validated by others will tend to be repressed or will simply fail to come into being**. If we are not seen, we cannot be fully alive.

So, the wish to be seen is quite understandable. On the other side of the coin, how, then, can we understand the FEAR of being seen? When we look deeply into this, we find at its core that we fear that we will discover that we are not worthy of being seen. In Buddhist terms, this is the **fear of non-being**. Our fear of being invisible connects both to our elemental fear of death and of existential emptiness. The fear of not being seen joins together with the fear of being alone, and can become the quest to fill our empty places with other people.

So it is useful to inquire deeply into both the wish and fear of being seen. We need to find within our own experience all the ways that, directly and indirectly, we seek Vitamin P. This includes all the constructive as well as dysfunctional ways we seek attention and approval. What we find is that our deepest desire is not for praise or approval, but for connection with others.

14

Inquiring Deeply About Emptiness

There is a not uncommon experience people allude to as "emptiness", meaning a deep sadness, yearning, or inner sense of something missing. It often connects to a felt sense of deep deficiency or unworthiness. This psychological emptiness is quite different in meaning from the Buddhist concept of the same name, which refers to the reality that things do not exist in the way we suppose that they do; that life is empty of anything which is inherently substantial or permanent enough for us to hold onto.

A good way to think about the psychological experience of emptiness is in terms of parts of us which have been lost from awareness. What has been lost from consciousness leaves a vacancy, a place which feels empty. Sometimes emptiness is a hole in our lives which comes from the loss of someone or something. It may arise in relation to something we want very badly but despair of ever finding/having. Psychic holes in the mind may also come about as a result of traumatic experience or something else barred from memory.

We can begin to explore emptiness by inquiring into the holes we find in our own lives. What is missing? In what way(s) do we feel insufficient? What emotions do we not want to feel? What in the balance of mind, body, and heart gets too little of our attention?

We can also explore emptiness by paying attention to what we do to "fill" the holes we feel within: our addictive attachments to substances, activities, and people. Ironically, our improvised "solutions" to pain most often result in new, worse problems! By exploring the strategies we use to block the feeling of what is painful, we can deepen our awareness of the underlying feelings.

When we turn our attention to exploring empty places within, often we may find memories of hurt feelings and conflicts that block our natural ability to connect to others. Our most habitual and powerful feelings and thoughts define the core of who we think we are. When we are caught up in a sense of being unworthy, the universal sense that "something is wrong" turns into the feeling that "something is wrong *with me.*" This felt sense keeps us on the run, driven by desperate efforts to get away from these bad feelings.

In a different vein, the experience of emptiness can sometimes be illuminated by contrasting it with its psychological opposite, aliveness. We can inquire about the experiences in which we have felt most whole and complete, most authentic, most at peace with ourselves and with our world. What has blocked these channels of vitality and aliveness?

In my view, our empty places, our "holes", can ultimately only be filled by connection: both connection with others and better connection to ourselves. Healing relationships (including psychotherapy) help us through deep listening both to what we say and what we don't say (and may never even have thought!). Deep empathic listening connects us heart-to-heart and cultivates our ability to extend compassion and tenderness towards what is wounded within us.

Mindful awareness of the experience of emptiness is a useful place to begin on the path of healing. If we have the inclination and/or interest, we may also find it useful at some point to contemplate the *emptiness* itself. In a philosophical/spiritual sense, "emptiness" points to the Everything/Nothing from which all manifestation arises. From this perspective, paradoxically, emptiness is a vast reservoir of unrealized potential.

In the words of the Taoist sage Lao Tzu, it is the emptiness within the cup that makes it useful.

Section III

The Relational Dimension of Change

15

The Relational Dimension of Emotional Experience

When we inquire deeply about our emotional reactions, we discover that very often what we react to emotionally is what other people have said or done (or *not* said/ *not* done) and the meanings that we have assigned to those things. With this in mind, deep inquiry investigates emotional reactions through the lens of our relationships with others. Not only do we gain a window of view into how relational events orchestrate our emotional lives, we begin to see that **our minds are organized subjectively around our connections with others.**

One important thing we can notice in the interplay between Self and Other is the repeated pattern of rupture — ideally followed by repair— between ourselves and others. We are constantly reactive to how well our interpersonal needs are met by others, and we are likely to experience emotional turbulence when they are not.

Understanding the dynamics between self and other is the primary domain of psychoanalysis. We all have psychological "complexes" (or "psychic knots" as I personally prefer to call them). In Jungian terms, this is the *shadow*. The shadow aspect of our personalities can be vividly observed in *"enactments"* with others: painful moments with romantic partners, family members, and friends which re-create in living color the psychological themes and patterns of early emotional life. We may get upset emotionally, and/or we may get stuck in repetitive, painful "knots" of entangled emotion and behavior (often in the form of fights) which are determined by the emotional baggage of both parties.

When difficult feelings or emotions are occurring, various psychological defenses may be engaged in order to avoid experiencing, admitting to, or dealing with unwanted feelings. One ubiquitous defense is that of **projection**, involving the attribution of one's own feelings to someone else. The unconscious aspect of personality is often revealed through this psychodynamic mechanism. It is not easy to know who is doing what to whom.

This becomes especially problematic when both people in a relationship have similar issues or knots. In a common enactment which occurs in couples, for example, both people feel wounded and angry at the same time and each perceives the other to have started it and to be at fault. The only way out of this cul de sac of mutual projection is for both people to be willing to step back and gain perspective on the fact that each person's patterns of attachment are challenged by the partner's. By gaining some perspective on the reactive pattern that is reciprocally triggered in one another, it becomes possible to come to an empathic understanding that is inclusive of the pain of both and free of blame.

This situation illustrates several primary dimensions of relationship boundaries. **Interpersonal boundaries** are usually defined as limits we set in regard to what is acceptable behavior on the part of ourselves or others. Many emotional upsets occur when one person fails to respect the boundaries set by the other, or when two people have a different idea about what appropriate boundaries should be. **Intersubjective boundaries** can be defined as invisible and fluctuating demarcations between where I leave off and you begin. The essence of both kinds of boundaries may be readily grasped by simile: what we see as happening on the "self" side of the street vs. what we take to be on the "other" side. Where self boundaries are poorly defined, we are liable to becoming entangled (enmeshed) with or defensively removed from others.

Bringing meditative awareness to our emotional upsets allows us to begin to penetrate the shadow with light by bringing attention to the unquestioned veracity of our perceptions. We need to understand that there is a quintessential ambiguity inherent in delineating who is doing what to whom. An important first step is acknowledging that interpersonal reality is always co-created. We are complicit in the construction of our subjective reality, and there is power in recognizing that there is also an underlying question: *"whose unconscious is it, anyway?"*[10]

Meditative inquiry about emotional reactivity provides a direct path to recognizing and understanding what is unhealed in our psyches. The very act of inquiring into what is happening entails a powerful and generative shift in awareness which allows us to begin to get unstuck from emotional reactivity. Contemplative rather than analytic in focus, the process of inquiry is one of posing questions and then *feeling our way* towards answers. Sitting with, being with, and repeatedly inquiring about who is doing what to whom is a means of inviting a profound shift in one's experience of the world. Deep inquiry enables us to discover how we are complicit in constructing our subjective world.

16

Relational Mindfulness and Relational Inquiry

Human beings are relational beings. We spend the majority of our lives conversing and interacting with others against a complex backdrop which includes the culture of our social connections. In a multitude of different ways, we are continually mixing minds with others (including in cyberspace). It is not an exaggeration to say that we are *made of* relationship. Relationship is the way we *inter-be* with others.

Relational inquiry can be broadly defined as the investigation of experiences that occur at the surfaces of our connection with others: the **"relational field"**. But there are many layers in the complex dance of human connection. We can delineate several different components of relatedness that fall within the scope of relational inquiry:

- **Interactions** are the behavioral events that occur between self and other. Some dimensions of interaction are *explicit*— what is said or done—and some are *implicit* or nonverbal. I liken the implicit dimension of interaction to the music of connection, behavior to the choreography of the dance.

- **Relational Mindfulness** is the moment-to-moment awareness *we bring to our experience of engaging with or interacting with someone.* The essence of relational mindfulness is simply noticing what is happening between ourselves and others. However, drawing from the paradigm of mindful awareness in Buddhist practice, relational mindfulness involves deliberately paying attention to the elements of thought, feeling, and body sensation that arise for us in the relational field and holding these experiences in nonjudgmental awareness.

  Relational mindfulness consists of layers of meaning organized around a **felt sense** of what it is like to *be with* a particular someone else; our embodied, whole person response to being with the other. Felt sense consists of the somatic and affective dimensions of experience.

- **Relational Inquiry**

  Emanating from the core felt sense, perceptions of the relational moment are elaborated based on our attachment history with others. For example, in some moments with others we may feel well received while in other moments the connection between us falls flat. Such interpersonal responses have deep roots in our past experiences. They are rooted in our needs for contact and connection as well as on our defensive needs for safety.

Relational inquiry is the introspective investigation of the interpersonal and psychodynamic dimensions of our encounters with others.

- **Relational Turbulence**

  It is informative to make a study of the things that upset us and that we are emotionally reactive to. Our psychological vulnerabilities are revealed most clearly in events that engage primal emotions such as anxiety, despondency, and shame; anger and blame; jealousy, envy, and competition; sexual attraction and lust. By intentionally paying attention to moments when we get interpersonally "hooked" or caught up in something someone did or said, we can glean valuable information about our unmet psychological needs; what we need to wake up to, and where we need to grow.

- **Speaking and Listening: the dance of communication**

  Because we spend so many hours of our lives talking to other people, conversation provides an especially rich opportunity for relational mindfulness. In conversation, we have the opportunity to listen to ourselves as well as to the listening of the other. We can see what we choose to say about ourselves and what this reflects about who we think we are.

We can observe our relational patterns. And, we have the opportunity to observe our reactivity as it happens.

There is a mysterious interpersonal chemistry that happens when we interact with others and "mix minds" in the relational field. Through the practice of relational inquiry, "inquiring deeply" about our interactions with others, we can become aware of the patterns involved in how our particular minds are organized around relationship and the issues which get in the way of our feeling free, spontaneous, and authentic with others.

Ultimately, relational inquiry enhances our self-understanding and our capacity to be intimate both with ourselves and with others. It supports us in staying present, open, and compassionate as life unfolds moment by moment. And, in so doing, it deepens our experience of being with others.

17

Reflections on Relationship as Dharma Practice

All of the essential truths of existence taught by the Buddha — "Buddhadharma"— are revealed in the phenomena of relationship. To mention just a few of the most salient:

- Like all phenomena, relational moments arise, morph, and evolve from moment to moment. Relationships are impermanent, in constant change. What we call *this relationship* is a conceptual composite of a multitude of relational moments.

- Interpersonal hunger and interpersonal aversion are sources of a great deal of human travail. Interpersonal suffering, like all suffering, arises from wishing things to be other than they are. We fail to recognize that relationships are inherently unreliable sources of satisfaction or happiness. The universal truth is that people often disappoint us, hurt us, or leave us, and even if they don't, eventually we will be parted by death.

- We often harbor mistaken or deluded views which govern our interactions with others. I call this realm of knowledge *"wise emotional understanding of relationship."*[11] It is helpful to be able to recognize the relational dynamics that underlie human behavior. Without empathic understanding of one another, we cannot optimize the opportunities for communication and connection between us.

- We mostly live in the fundamental illusion that we are separate beings, whereas, in truth, everything we consider to be our "self" can readily be shown to be intrinsically dependent upon its relational context.

Because we are relational beings, frequently beset with interpersonal "dukkha", it is skillful to be able to bring dharma practice and relational experience together in one frame. This is fundamentally what I mean by "inquiring deeply": awareness practice which focuses on our interactions and connections with others. With this kind of inquiry, we come to **emotional understandings which are broad enough and deep enough to encompass both psyche and dharma**.

The primary observation is that the mind organizes itself in and for relationship. Our entire paradigm of personal meanings derives from an interpersonal framework. Relational themes infuse the way we relate to our own bodies and minds and even to the very process of how we relate to life itself.

Inquiring Deeply About Relationship

"Relational mindfulness" is the practice of bringing mindful awareness into the interpersonal domain. It begins by becoming aware of the basic features of our lived experience in the presence of others: our body sensations, breath, feelings, and the associative network of thoughts that accompany them.

But more than simply denuded moments of mindful awareness, each relational moment also has its own felt sense of closeness/intimacy; or, conversely, emotional distance. In some moments with others, we may feel well received while in other moments the connection between us falls flat. Our tendency to move towards or away from a particular relational moment depends on our current needs for contact and connection, our deepest feelings of vulnerability, and our defensive needs for safety. **Mindfulness of connection** is a window of view into this basic interpersonal and psychodynamic dimension of relationship.

With self-reflection, relational mindfulness becomes a stage for observing the **"theatre of the mind"**. One primary observation is that interpersonal dramas tend to occupy center stage in our minds. Plotlines revolve around who is doing what to whom. We can see this both in the melodramas of everyday life as well as in the epic dramas of social injustice, political intrigue, and war that unfold in the body politic. All involve familiar interpersonal themes of love and loss; violation and betrayal; conquest and defeat. We can gain psychological self-understanding by paying attention to these themes as they are reflected in the stories we tell (either to ourselves or to others) about "what happened" or "what is happening." And, by transforming our narratives, we can also transform ourselves.

It is informative to make a study of the things that upset us and that we are emotionally reactive to. Our psychological vulnerabilities are revealed most clearly in events that engage primal emotions such as anxiety, despondency, and shame; anger and blame; jealousy, envy, and competition; sexual attraction and lust. By intentionally paying attention to moments when we get interpersonally "hooked" or caught up in something someone did or said (or failed to do/say) we can glean valuable information about our unmet psychological needs.

In addition, there is a lot to be learned by exploring the way we "show up" in the dramas of our lives. Not only are we different with particular others, we are different scene by scene. It is interesting to observe the different self-states (subpersonalities) we express in different moments and reflect on where these come from in us. One basic insight is that we are made of relational building blocks. After all, we modeled ourselves after the people we experienced most closely in childhood. Through the practice of relational inquiry, we can locate our identifications with these ghosts from the past in our current behavior, including posture, mannerisms, and gestures. We see ourselves most clearly through the lens of the relationships we form with others.

Abundant opportunities for interpersonal dharma practice are available if we make it a practice to be alert to the emotional reactivity that can happen any time we come into contact with others. The inevitable conflicts and difficulties in human interactions are rich sources of understanding and insight into what governs human motivation and behavior. This is especially true between primary partners, where relationship exposes areas of vulnerability and psychological wounding. Areas of mutual reactivity can explode in ways which are painful but which have the potential to reveal both where we are stuck and where we need to grow.

As we reflect on the dynamics that have arisen between ourselves and others, we can investigate the truth that it always takes two to tango— that all events that occur between self and other are actually *co-arising*. This begins to broaden our view beyond a self-focused perspective (self-view) to a relational view.

Summary and Conclusions:

The tendency to get caught up in painful entanglements with others is a basic aspect of our human nature. For those of us to like to "work on ourselves", relationships are a perfect path for awareness practice. They wake us up to the complex construction of self and other, and, in so doing, help us recognize that what we find when we look inward and what we see when we look outward are not separate, but rather mutually reflective surfaces of experience. This is the penetrating truth of **interbeing**: everything is interrelated and constituted by its matrix of connections with everything else.

Relationally-focused dharma practice supports us in staying present, open, and compassionate as life unfolds moment by moment. Ultimately, its goal is to evoke and enhance our capacity to live from the quality of relatedness that the philosopher Martin Buber called **"I-Thou"**: The ability to connect to one another from that place of deep being that lives behind our eyes, one whole human being to another, subject to subject.

18

Wise Relationship:
9th Step on the Eightfold Noble Path

Relational angst is one of the primary sources of pain in this human life. While personal stresses derive principally from our interactions with family members, coworkers, and friends, our psychological dysfunctions also seem increasingly to be permeating the larger socio-cultural whole. Indeed, in my view our collective mental health seems generally to have been in a state of decline in recent years, accelerating in its downward trajectory during the pandemic and with the stressors of our recent national political climate.

Psychological, interpersonal, and social suffering are deeply interwoven. In Buddhist terms, it is all *dukkha*: part of our universal and essential human dissatisfaction with the terms of human existence. Consistent with what the Buddha taught, it is quite obviously true that greed, hatred, and ignorance are at the root of our relational suffering. Equally obvious, our individual well-being is interconnected with the well-being of all. For these reasons, I believe that it behooves each of us to inquire deeply about the true meaning of "wise relationship." In so doing, not only can we relieve our own suffering, but in some small way, perhaps, we may also mitigate the suffering of the collective.

Although wise relationship is implicit in all limbs of the eightfold noble path (for example, in the applications of right view, intention, action, and speech), Buddhist psychology does not explicitly address the nature of the relational entanglements that give rise to most of our difficulties. If anything, Buddhism tends to point us towards not getting entangled in such things, warning of how readily we can get lost in them. There is merit in taking this caution to heart: personal relationships present formidable challenges. We should all be chastened by the conspicuous examples of otherwise wise teachers who have gotten caught up in very unwise relationships!

* * * * * * *

So, a good preliminary inquiry is: *What Is a "Wise Relationship?"* Contemplating this question can go in many different directions all at once. It may include ideas about what is virtuous and wholesome, such as those elaborated in Buddhist teachings, but it is also meant to elicit a deeper understanding of what wise relationship is and how we recognize when it is present.

In a very general sense, if we aspire to *engage* wise relationship, it is helpful to begin from inside: reflecting on your own experience of wise relationship.

> *Set your mind to recall times that you have felt like you were in the presence of relating wisely with others: either some way that you felt wise, or some way that you have been on the receiving end of someone else's wisdom.*
>
> *Recall any parables, teaching stories, or similar that evoke wise relationship for you.*

For me, the quintessence of "wise relationship" seems to go to the subjective quality of being with someone; a felt sense. What we can notice is that sometimes it simply feels clear that we are in the presence of wisdom and compassion. When we are interacting with others, there is a deeply felt sense of intimacy and presence. Sometimes we may feel a sense of channeling wisdom, compassion, or both, which feels very enlivening.

The very same relationship may feel very wise in some moments and very fraught in others. But then, is that really the same relationship? [Can you really step in the same river twice?]

* * * * * * *

I find it useful to think of wise relationship as a kind of three-legged race. When there is cooperation, resonance, and synchrony between us, things move along well. When there is not — when instead we encounter a reaction which impedes us — an "entanglement"— we need to examine the disruption and find a wise path forward towards repair. To invoke Phillip Moffitt's evocative phrase, we need to practice "dancing with life", and, as the saying goes, when you stumble, make it part of the dance.

* * * * * * *

Entanglements, and the problems that result from them, ultimately stem from our interpersonal reactivity and its emotional roots.

Such human difficulties are not optional! Most of us have little or no education about, nor modeling of, how to understand the dynamics between people in relationship nor how to wisely engage the difficulties.

Deep investigation and inquiry can help to illuminate the nature of the entanglements we find ourselves in, and by our willingness to engage with our problems in this way, the path of wise relationship reveals itself. This kind of inquiry is well suited to psychological problems, and some of what we learn is applicable to the understanding of sociocultural conflict as well.

In this and the next series of Inquiring Deeply Newsletters, my intention is to describe a path of contemplative inquiry about Wise Relationship in the form of some questions that can be useful to practice with. I regard such inquiry less as a formal practice than as a creative process; a way of *practicing with psychological problems*. Simply put, in the process of *inquiring deeply* I pose questions (for myself or to others) as a means of feeling my way into the emotional core of the entanglement.

Asking basic questions of ourselves or others in the face of relational turbulence helps to illuminate what is occurring: what expectations have been disappointed, what psychological needs have been thwarted, or what other difficulty is present.

Fundamentally, deep inquiry is less about the particular questions that we ask than about the way that we listen for the answers. As Albert Einstein wisely said, we cannot solve a problem from the same level of consciousness that created it. We inquire deeply as a way of shifting the way that we relate to our process of relating with others. Questions are a chrysalis in which solutions to our relational problems slowly develop and emerge.

19

Entanglements:
Who Is Doing What To Whom?

The Calm at the Center of the Storm

As has been explored in previous issues of this Newsletter, human beings are relational beings.

Relationships are the source of our greatest joys in life, and yet, paradoxically, also the source of our greatest suffering. Both are an important topics for meditative exploration and contemplation. Bringing Presence to the intimate edge of our connection with others can be revealing, and it holds the potential to transform how we relate.

Relational inquiry is broad in scope. For example, we can explore who we like/dislike, and why. (And what exactly is entailed in "liking someone?") We can notice what parts of ourselves show up in particular situations; what feelings and psychological needs come up; what is it that wants/needs to be known or spoken. Following the guidelines of Buddhist practice, we can investigate the surface of our connection with others both externally (what is occurring between us) and internally (how we are holding the relationship in mind).

Here I want to focus on a particular set of relational difficulties in close relationships that we may call **entanglement**. I am not using this term as a euphemism for a dysfunctional connection with someone, but rather to point to repetitive painful "knots" of entangled emotion (often in the form of fights) which are determined by the emotional baggage of both parties. This can become especially problematic when both people in the relationship have similar psychological issues — which is often the case because such vulnerabilities are part of what attracts us to particular others in the first place.

A very common entanglement is that which occurs when both people feel wounded and/or angry at the same time and each blames the other for having started it. (A pervasive dynamic in couples!) This is by its very nature a reactive situation, and the anger and/or pain that arises can be emotionally destabilizing.

What are skillful means for dealing with entanglements such as this? In the usual application of mindfulness practice to the situation, the general "prescription" goes by the acronym R.A.I.N.: recognition, acceptance, investigation, and non-identification.[12] In order to see the truth of what is happening, it is recommended that we pause the reactive pattern and drop the story in order to go beneath the surface level of the moment which is clouded with emotions and habitual thinking.

But finding our way past the cul de sac of entanglement is also helped by deepening our emotional understanding of how each person's patterns of attachment are challenged by the partner's. More than simple awareness, and beyond cognitive understanding of the situation, we need to feel our way into the upset. I often liken this to how we feel for a splinter at the center of an area of inflammation on the skin. True transformation of entanglements depends on our ability to truly meet the emotional challenge on its own terms.

Inquiring deeply into the question *"who is doing what to whom?"* can begin to detangle the situation. Our initial idea of what is happening needs to include, for example, the recognition that whatever is happening is a *co-arising event.* To see the relational difficulty in terms of *we* instead of *you* vs. *me* is itself an important step forward.

Often the best place to begin to see more deeply into *"who is doing what to whom?"* is in contemplation after the fact. Once the upset has passed and we have recovered our self-reflective function, we can step back and try to gain some perspective on the reactive pattern that each of us reciprocally triggers in the other. A period of open-awareness sitting meditation provides a good opportunity to see more clearly what is going on for us. What comes up in awareness helps to reveal what we are defending, what we need to be right about, and what is at stake.

The inquiry question *"who is doing what to whom?"* may show us the relational roots of the reactive pattern we are caught in. Associations to earlier similar experiences in family of origin or in other relationships may be explored. Which actual others did what to you (or someone else) ? And/or, is this something *you* have ever done to someone else? It is helpful to learn to notice more clearly when we engage psychological defenses in order to avoid experiencing, admitting to, or dealing with unwanted feelings. Ideally, by examining the pattern and its network of associations in the mind, we can come to an empathic understanding of the entanglement that is inclusive of the pain of both partners and free of blame.

The question of "*who is doing what to whom?*" is a good inquiry practice. In the heat of difficult interactions with others, simply engaging with this question may sometimes help us to get free from whatever relational box we have gotten trapped in. There is calm at the center of every relational storm where we can remind ourselves to look for what it is we love in this person we are upset with and where we can remember our relational aspirations.

At a deeper level, inquiring deeply into "*who is doing what to whom?*" can help to free us from the ego identifications that keep us stuck. Relational entanglements can show us the living reality that we are intersubjective beings in a constant and fluid process of relational exchange with others. Experiential awareness of this "interbeing" holds the key to transformation of entanglement.

20

Resolving Entanglements With Inquiry

Emotional pain is truth knocking on a door that
has been closed too long"

—Anonymous

As described in the previous issue, *entanglements* are repetitive is-sues or conflicts that arise in close relationships, causing emotional upset — *"relational turbulence."* Though the focus in the previous discussion was on dynamics between intimate partners, entangle-ments also occur in relationships between family members, friends, and co-workers — in many (if not all) of our connections with others.

They are the source of much of the psychological distress in life.

Entanglements arise as a function of the emotional baggage we carry. We experience relationship in a context which includes our memories of similar situations in the past where we were hurt, disappointed, invalidated, rejected, or even abused. Because of these reactions, as the writer William Faulkner famously said, "The past is never dead. It's not even past." This basic fact of psychological life readily gives rise to blurring in our minds (and in our experience) about relational turbulence. In that state of mind, emotional chaos may make it hard to be clear about what happened then vs. what is happening now, and about who is doing what to whom.

Entanglements are made worse when the personal boundaries of the participants are undifferentiated, permeable, or unclear. Each person may then become liable to psychological enmeshment with the other, unproductively involved with the other's emotional reactions. Each one is triggered by the other. In this state of mutual reactivity, both people will tend to feel on the receiving end of something unpleasant, trapped in a familiar relational box. **This reciprocal entanglement in repetitive painful patterns of interaction forecloses the possibility that something new will occur**.

Unfortunately, there is no simple formula for resolving these kinds of situations. The process of resolving entanglements is just that: a *process*. Relationship is a path we are travelling with another, and difficulties on the path are best approached with the mindset of being aware and looking for what may be constructive in going forward. I liken this process to the way we might travel through fog: by slowing down and feeling our way forward step by step. When I am in this situation, I try to wrap my mind around surrendering to the situation with the intention to find an opening. But everyone needs to find their own way. The basic aspiration is simply to bring kind attention to the relational surfaces that are painful or difficult for us.

Having recognized that we are caught up in an entanglement with someone, the experiential priority is to pause: to *stop* and *feel*. What is this experience like for you? What might it be like for the Other? Inquire deeply. This is a moment when there is something for you to discover; something that needs to be known.

Simply recognizing that we are caught in an entanglement is the essential first step. In that recognition, we move into the position of witness — analogous to what in Zen is called a "backward step." Such moments provide the beginning of insight into the true nature of an entanglement: In order to accept the other person, we must first see more clearly what it is that their actions trigger in us. We need to ask ourselves "what feeling within myself am I having trouble being with?" To the extent that we get caught up in a reaction to someone else, we become blind to the part of the difficulty that lies within ourselves.

The relational field is an important mirror in which we have the opportunity to deeply encounter ourselves and others. Such moments are important stepping stones on each person's path of spiritual and psychological growth. They hold the promise of all that is not yet known.

21

Irreconcilable Differences

Generally speaking, we seek agreement with our significant others, but differences are inevitable. In the interest of "wise relationship" it behooves us to understand what constitutes "irreconcilable differences" and how best to relate to them.

In simple terms, I define an "irreconcilable difference" as any interpersonal issue which puts the viability of the relationship in question— something which causes intractable conflict and for which no solution can be found. But when we look closely at such situations, often we find that the issue is less about the substance of the difference than it is about how both people are reacting to one another. Beyond the content of so-called irreconcilable differences, there is generally something about the other that each is unable to accept. It is wise to look beyond the disagreement to the reactive process underneath.

In previous issues of this Newsletter, I unpacked some aspects of our reactions that are due to the complex web of psychological/emotional/relational conflicts that I call entanglements. Here I want to focus on the nature of differences in values, opinions, and beliefs; to differences in subjective "truth."

Of course, how we relate to our differences is as much about our psychological and emotional patterns as it is about our points of view. We have very different "windows of tolerance" for differences. In one couple I worked with, for example, different tastes in music and preference for how loud music should be played in their home had become a domestic war. Recently I have worked with several couples who struggle with finding middle ground between troubling differences in political views. In seeking to help couples work through disagreements, I try to help them see clearly where they are stuck and what is at stake for each of them.

The crux of the matter often seems to boil down to a conflict over whose view is **right** and whose view is **wrong**. All of us tend to assume (and prefer to think) that our views are correct, and we get very invested in our positions about things. After all, our views construct the reality we live in, and the need for reality to be coherent is a primary psychological need. In such situations, it is useful to see clearly what it is we are trying to be right about and why that is important to us. It is also useful to look for instances of black and white thinking. Both/And is a much wiser frame than Either/Or!

Polarized disagreements often devolve into fights which involve negative judgment and blame— basic manifestations of anger. In examining this relational pattern closely in many couples, what I have invariably found is that someone, or both someones, are certain that they are right. The attitude of moral superiority that creeps into such disagreements is one of the most common emotional stumbling blocks between significant others.

For me, as I think for many of us, an attitude of **righteousness** in others is one of the most difficult personality characteristics to be with. There is value in inquiring deeply about this until we begin to discern clearly the shadow of the same righteousness within ourselves. The need to be right is a basic aspect of the way we defend cherished views of ourselves; views that we are very identified with and invested in.

In considering how to respond wisely to disagreements with others, I have also found it valuable to reflect on a quote attributed to the film director Federico Fellini: *"Happiness is being able to tell the truth without hurting anyone."* What "truth" is it that we think we need to tell?

As a preliminary step, we are wise to understand that what we consider to be "the truth" is subjectively determined and therefore necessarily subject to disagreement. One of the basic things that I have learned in working with people in psychotherapy is that, **regardless of its objective validity, subjective truth needs to be understood/validated**. If we look deeply enough, what we can find is that everyone has good and sufficient reasons for taking the positions that they do; for their behavior and for their beliefs. Right vs. wrong is a very limiting frame. However, that does <u>not</u> mean that we should regard all truths as equally valid. There are outer limits to what points of view we can regard as sane, and our respect for the reality of others will necessarily be constrained by what we consider to be crazy (or even dangerous). Nonetheless, communication is well served in any conflict by the sincere intention to see and empathize with the other's point of view.

Another basic observation is that hearing our truth will feel uncomfortable to someone who doesn't wish to accept it. Beyond the need to be right, we all want to maintain a positive view of ourselves, and it can be painful to take in the negative view that someone else may hold. But notwithstanding that criticism may be painful for someone to hear, it also provides an important opportunity. (In the vernacular, an "AFGO" — another f-cking growth opportunity!)

Consider, moreover, that there is a risk in <u>not</u> speaking my truth as well as in speaking it. For though it may hurt you for me to tell you my truth about you, it may also be unwise for me to protect *your* feelings at the expense of abdicating my own.

A good general strategy when we find ourselves in intractable conflict with another is to back off as much as necessary to restore (or find anew) the "highest common ground." At the intersection of our differences, it is also helpful to practice what I have called elsewhere the "intimate dance of speaking and listening."[13] Beyond cultivating communication skills, deep listening is a way to deepen the intimacy of our interaction and invite the unfolding of a mutual experience of being known. Beneath the surface of conflict, there is a lot we can learn about the common humanity of our vulnerability; of our wish to be seen, our fear of being seen, and our wish to connect deeply with others.

If, as Fellini suggests, happiness is being able to tell the truth, we also need to recognize that wise relationship entails not just speaking but **living** our subjective truth. "Should I leave?" is an important question, and living in the question of whether our differences are irreconcilable is a complex challenge. "Irreconcilable differences" are a way-station that may arise on the path that people sometimes travel when they are seeking to emancipate themselves from bonds with others which they find to be shackling. However, as Buddhist teacher and psychologist Jack Kornfield reminds us, while it may feel necessary to distance ourselves from another person for a while or forever, it is never necessary to put anyone out of our hearts. In other words, we don't need to use irreconcilable differences to justify our need to separate.

Instead, wise relationship invites us to speak, act, and live our lives, not from reactive patterns, but from the "wisdom inside the growing capacity to pause, reflect, and connect with choice."[14] While we may not be able to **resolve** a disagreement, we can usually find a way to **reconcile** by appropriately adjusting our boundaries and interpersonal distance. The quality of our relationships rests upon the foundation of our wise understanding and the kindness of our intentions.

Section IV

Coming Into Being

22

On Being Oneself

"Today you are you, that is truer than true.
There is no one alive who is you-er than you."

—Dr. Seuss

The curious fact is that it's not always easy to just "be yourself", nor even to know precisely who that *is*. "Who Am I?" is one of the most basic questions we can ask in deep meditative inquiry. This question first appeared in my awareness when I was three years old and it is still alive in me.

We can address this question at various levels of depth, both

intellectually and experientially. I can convey some basic points of my understanding by describing the experience I had several decades ago at a contemplative inquiry retreat. The inquiry took place in a dyadic dialogue format. In each 45 minute segment, one partner simply gave the prompt: "tell me who you are", while the other partner contemplated, answered, and then contemplated some more. We reversed roles. Then we changed partners.
For a total of 54 hours.

Of the many things that happened for me during this profound retreat, one vivid element I recall was the sensory experience of the collective voices in the room. The first night was marked by the sounds of lively chatter as everyone told their story: (What I do for a living, who I'm married to, what I studied in school, what I do for fun, where I live, etc.) By the second day, the collective mind had become very much more settled. There was a lot of silence in the room as well as a palpable sense of meditative presence. (Similarly in my own mind: a lot of stillness, with empty space between thoughts).

While it was interesting in its own right to observe the content of what came up for me in response to the prompt, eventually it all seemed to boil down to the feeling of "*blah, blah, blah*": a kind of boredom I felt about the oft-told story of myself (or maybe even a certain boredom with self itself.) I gained a deep appreciation of a truth articulated by the psychoanalyst Roy Schafer: **"The self is a story; it is the story that there is a self to tell a story to."** [15]

At the same time, it was also clear that behind the story of Who I Am — beneath the layers of identity and personality — there was a **felt experience** of *what it is like to be me.* (Who am I? I'm *me!*) This felt sense was ineffable, but somehow constant behind fluid and continuously changing subjective experience. I felt a profound sense of realization regarding the truth of Heraclitus' well-known aphorism "you can't step in the same river twice." (It wouldn't be the same river, nor would it be the same person.) And yet, there was also an indisputable experience of sameness within the subjective diversity: a sense of **"me."** This subjective experience is what we call the **psychological self** (the being of which is the topic of this discussion.)

Looking back from my current vantage point, several decades later, my sense is that becoming myself has been a lifelong process of deepening **authenticity**. Though difficult to define, authenticity refers generally to the congruence between what we say/do and who we are. Simply put, I am authentic when I am being myself (so at this point the definition becomes circular). Nonetheless, broadly speaking, authenticity is reflected in how we inhabit ourselves; how comfortable we feel in our own skins; by our spontaneity and freedom of expression. It also carries the meaning that we are fulfilling our innate potential.

In contrast, we are *inauthentic* when we show up in a way that forfeits individual meaning in favor of the habit of trying to please and accommodate the wishes of others. In this case, the natural, spontaneous expression of "who we are" gets co-opted. "False Self" supplants "True Self."

The ability to authentically be oneself is reflected by how we show up in life. It has to do with how we relate to ourselves as well as with our ability to be vulnerable and intimate with others. It is an evolving dimension of being increasingly comfortable and natural, as expressed by the following great quote: *"I used to be different, now I'm the same."*[16]

The quality and depth of being which is engaged when I am *being myself* is the quintessential thing. The ideal state of being entails an experience of flow as well as a sense of being optimally tuned and responsive to what is going on both internally and externally. We feel alert and aware; subjectively cohesive, alive, and integrated. This is what I call, for want of a better phrase, "true subjectivity." In some moments, this experience may deepen into stillness, a sense of mystery, or even awe: ultimately, the ineffable experience of being itself. In such moments, we come home to ourselves.

23

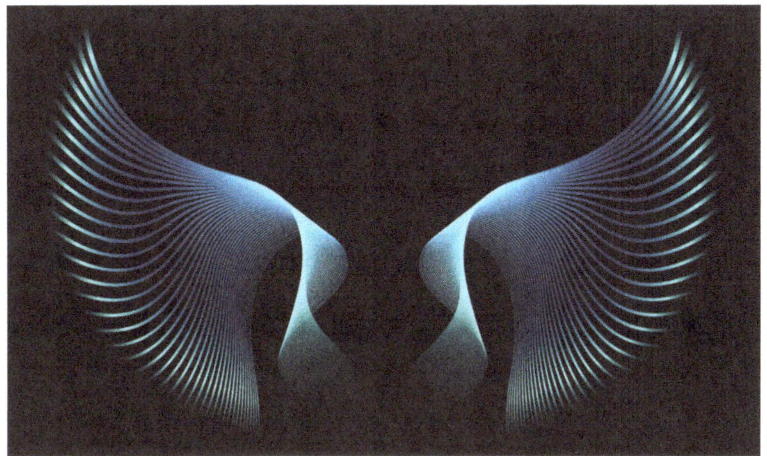

In Pursuit of Inner Freedom

A friend recently asked me what I was planning to write about next. I said that I didn't know, except that my intention was to not plan it; instead, I wanted to give my writing a chance to unfold; to emerge from within. Fundamentally, the essence of this creative process is identical with the orientation towards *inner knowing* which is cultivated in the practice of meditation. It has three interrelated aspects: 1) the intention to *receive* experience in lieu of any effort to manage or control it; 2) the commitment to allocate time, space, and energy to writing; and 3) an attitude of *trust* towards whatever would emerge as a consequence of #1 and #2.

I knew that my ability to write clearly, like my ability to discern clearly, often depends upon how well I am able to clear the clutter or confusion in my mind at any given moment. If I could appropriately settle myself to write, much as I try to do when engaging in a process of contemplative inquiry, I trusted that what I was looking for would appear.

Ironically, having articulated and written that one thought, I recognized that a new piece of writing had, in fact, just begun. Beginning with the question of *"What do I want to write next?"*, my first discovery was that the answer to this question was best revealed to me through the process of engaging in the act of writing. In this way, **the activity of writing became an embodied act of inquiry unto itself.**

Second, as I have written elsewhere, posing an inquiry question is a powerful act.[17] The question serves as a kind of intentional matrix of meaning which serves to support growth and facilitate the emergence of new experience. Because I have struggled with a feeling of inner tyranny, this inquiry was an appropriate "practice" for me.

As I immersed myself in the process of writing, a set of contemplative reflections started to crystallize in my mind as fractals of a lifetime of interrelated thoughts about the nature of inner freedom. First, I saw quite clearly that my quest for inner freedom has been one of the central repeating themes of my life. Simultaneously, the pattern of psychological obstacles I have encountered in my lifelong pursuit of this freedom became clear. The metaphor of "fractals" seemed perfect, implying as it does that the questions we face and the choices we make are self-similar in the different levels of our lives, our behavior, and our psyches.

Freedom *from* has mostly been something I have struggled with in relation to the constant demands of my professional striving and what I have termed the *"tyranny of the to do list."* Freedom *to* has mostly lived for me as a quest for the highly valued experience of spacious awareness familiar to me from meditation practice. In either case, the pursuit of freedom needs to begin by exploring the ways that we *don't* feel free. In the words of the familiar Zen saying, "the obstacle is the path." Obstacles are not what stands in our way; they are the way itself.

A basic layer of the core of the issue for me has to do with how I typically manage the *Doing* of life, including functions such as defining goals, planning and prioritizing tasks, and similar. "Planning Mind" is a useful shorthand for these various executive functions. I am highly organized by nature, most at home within a framework of schedules and To Do lists. I am oriented toward working hard at everything I do. This allows me to be productive but, alas, this personal m.o. is not conducive to receptively allowing anything!

In writing an essay, for example, the good student in me readily goes to work generating outlines and bullet points. While this kind of structure is not optimal in regard to freedom of self-expression, I can also recognize that my analytical mind often comes up with a lot of creative ideas, so I try to avoid throwing out the baby with the bathwater. Where does this leave me? With the challenge to find a balance between being proactive and directed, on the one hand, and receptive and allowing on the other.

There are several interrelated layers of psychological issues. The way we relate to Time is central. To be too much in a hurry, beset with deadlines, too pressured or impatient for results, is a hindrance to contemplative writing. The Buddha used the simile of the lute to illustrate the concept of right effort: strings which are tuned either too tight or too loose interfere with the quality of the music that the instrument can make. In regard to time, the most useful self-guidance is to Slow Down. This takes a lot of practice but is a very worthy contemplative aspiration.

In order to deepen my inquiry about the tyranny of time in my life, I recently devoted four days to a meditation "staycation" (self-retreat) in order to explore how scheduling lives in my experience. In order to deepen my experience of the *non-doing* which is meditation, I deliberately decided in advance *not* to predetermine my schedule of practice: not to choose in advance of the actual moment what practice I would do in that period of practice (sitting meditation, walking meditation, yoga, etc.) I thought of this as an extension of the idea of open-focus awareness practice: Instead of a pre-determined schedule of practice, I would simply investigate how "free choice" actually unfolded from moment to moment and over the days of the retreat. Many of the ideas about subjective experience of freedom explored in this essay became clearer to me during those days of retreat practice.

Gradually The Pursuit of Freedom became my contemplative focus in this essay. It was apparent to me that the crux of the issue is the structure of our inner tyrannies: that which makes us hold on so tightly to what we are doing/feel that we need to do. We all have basic needs for safety, love, and belonging; the need to be in control, solve problems, and stay safe. Other things being equal, we become organized around the pursuit of whatever we think will make us happy: pleasure, success, power, money, status, relationships, and so on. The tyranny of striving rests on deeply embedded aspects of character which make us vulnerable to states of inner angst. For example, we may feel anxious about whether we will be able to get what we need; or, we may feel driven to try to get more of whatever it is, driven by the fear that we won't be able to get enough.

There are endless variations. As a starting point, it is helpful for people to see clearly what it is that they are trying to be, do, or have.

In some form or another, most of us are caught up in trying to be in control of something we are not in control of. Often, we are consciously or unconsciously trying to "fix it" (or fix ourselves).

When this predicament reveals itself, a common next reaction is: "*So how do I stop doing that?*" as if it were something that we needed *to do*. Just as we cannot "fall ourselves to sleep" at night, what is wanted and needed in regard to many of our problems is, instead, the *absence* of our customary *doing*. When possible, we can make a different choice. But, in general, what we need to "do" is simply to see more clearly what we are holding tightly to or trying to control, and, as best we are able, relax into the predicament.

Easy to say but hard to do. (Actually, not something which can be *done* at all!)

Regardless of what our particular pursuit may be, the essence of inner tyranny is that we get stuck in defining the meaning of our lives in terms of completions which live in the future. This is a true predicament, in that you simply can't get there from here. Seeking stands in the way of finding.

Along similar lines, although you can *be* happy, you can't **get** happy.

Conclusions

Those who have followed my work or who know me personally will recognize that what I have written here is fundamentally what I have learned as I have inquired deeply about "workaholism."[18] Writing this issue of INQUIRING DEEPLY NEWSLETTER has been a marvelous vehicle for that self-exploration/ inquiry. What is conceptualized on these pages has articulated and validated some insights which have been in the process of unfolding in me for some time.

The overarching ongoing theme is, I think, my quest for internal freedom through a shift from Doing to Being. There is a beautiful challenge in holding this intention without making it into a pursuit of some future attainment. In the most rewarding of such moments, the experience of freedom lives in me both as an appreciation of the perfection of *What Is* as well as an opening into an unlimited sense of possibility.

24

Listened Into Being

I have long been a proponent of what the poet David Whyte calls the "conversational nature of reality." What we articulate and communicate to one another has power; in the conversational mirror of the other, we gain access to the freedom to think new thoughts and to see ourselves in new ways. This gives conversation an enormous potential to deepen our experience and even transform our identity.

However, not just any conversation will do. As I observe this process in my own experience, it seems to me that in addition to a pre-requisite interpersonal resonance, I need to feel that my listener has the capacity to understand what I am trying to say in a deep way. It is only when I feel "well met" by another that a truly generative conversation is likely to happen.

There are as many different kinds of conversation as there are people or topics to talk about, but I highlight the following dimensions that seem to invite generative or transformative dialogue:

- First, **the quality of connection is key**. In much the same way that particular characteristics of children are brought forth by what their parents see and respond to in them, we continue to transform throughout life in response to the interactions and conversations we have with others. (In one such relationship, my friend told me that she felt like I was a thirsty plant that, for whatever reason, she had a talent for watering).

- Second, **dialogue can be enhanced as a function of the intention(s) that each of us brings to the conversation**. I prize most highly those conversations in which I engage with someone(s) in deep inquiry around some particular question of interest. Psychotherapy is one example of such a specialized conversation. Its intersubjective magic happens, I believe, when we have the intention to provide a healing relational environment for the other and when we are able to see both who the other *is* and what is standing in his or her way.

- Third, **the power of the dialogue we share with others is a function of the depth of Presence brought to the process of listening**. Contemplative dialogue *can* be structured around topics decided in advance but it need not be. We can simply engage one another in a process of discovery about something of interest, where we listen for what wants to be said and known at the tip of the current moment.

In what follows, I describe a deep inquiry that I have been engaged with in dialogue with a dharma colleague. I had a specific goal for this inquiry: to overcome the inhibitions that stand in the way of my freedom of self-expression as a writer. I articulated my purpose or aspiration as *finding the authentic voice of my own wisdom*. As described in the bullet points above, my belief was that simply by engaging in this inquiry and encountering the inhibitions that arose, the entire matter of **authenticity** would get clarified for me; and it was.

Here are some of the main ideas that informed the inquiry that unfolded:

- Since one of the central premises in my practice of inquiry is that answers unfold in response to the questions that we ask, I began to reflect deeply about what my important questions were. I knew that the general area was self-doubt. But what were the *specific* things I felt inhibited to speak about? And why?

- I could best find the answers I needed by entering into conversation and seeing what views and opinions I felt reluctant to express. Ironically, I already knew that *inquiry itself* would be the hardest thing to talk about, because that is my leading edge at this time and is what I am challenging myself to articulate in writing.

- I felt that it would be valuable to think out loud with others —especially with others I respect as discerning and astute— in order to see where the holes in my thinking might lie and in order to gain greater clarity and confidence. (This was one of the conscious intentions I had when I began to meet with this particular colleague.)

- I have in the past opined that thinking, like language, is essentially a relational act, but in our shared dialogue, this became increasingly and abundantly clear: *Often I don't even know what I think in advance of hearing what I have to say!*

- The emergence of "answers" and insights in the process of our inquiry/dialogue were often heralded by my feeling anxious or upset following a conversation. When those feelings came up, my effort was simply to feel my way into whatever was most sharp and uncomfortable. Often, this process found its way into my meditation sittings, where clarity would emerge.

- I gained considerable conceptual clarity in these conversations. But beyond ideas, what emerged for me was also a feeling of being able to rest in the process of dialogue and in the truth that thinking actually **is** a relational act. Though I had described this process before, I now felt that I could "put my money where my mouth was" and trust that this conversation was one which could hold me. I could **rest in the relationality of thinking!**

What stands out for me in hindsight is how much braver I have become over time about expressing my ideas. As I reflect on why this is so, what strikes me is that it has to do with the risks I have taken in allowing myself to be vulnerable; my willingness to reveal my ignorance and to disclose parts of myself that I tend to guard. In short, this conversational arena gave me lots of chances to *show up as myself,* and in so doing has allowed me to grow more comfortable in my own skin.

In short, by repeatedly making the choice to be vulnerable and to communicate authentically, I planted seeds which were able to blossom into flowers of mutual understanding and greater self-acceptance. This to me is the essence of how we listen one another into being.

"Each friend represents a world in us, a world possibly not born until they arrive, and it is only by this meeting that a new world is born."

—Anais Nin

25

The Hunger For Deep Conversation

I have recently been reflecting on the process I go through in the course of "inquiring deeply" about something. In the beginning, a topic generally feels less like something I choose than like something which chooses me. I have likened the process to getting pregnant: the implanting of an idea which begins to grow within me. Early on, most often I will have a felt sense of urgency about it, that there is something which is important to me to understand, although I don't at first know what the need is about. So my inquiries generally begin with my recognizing a familiar experience of urgency or agitation, followed by my effort to discover where the emotional charge is coming from in me.

To further my process, I may often initiate conversation with others about it, until at some point it feels as though my thoughts "ask" to be written down. At this point, the inquiry transitions into written form. It then matures over the course of successive written drafts until finally I feel satisfied by the meaning which has taken shape and a new issue of this Newsletter is born.

The inquiry which is currently compelling my attention is the **nature of the hunger for deep conversation** —an aspect of the urgency referenced above. I can sense that there is something within me which wants/needs to be understood, something which feels important. My previous writings illustrate earlier phases of my inquiry about this— (e.g. "*On The Importance of Being Understood*" — this volume, Section II; "*Speaking and Listening: The Intimate Dance of Communication*[13]"). At the heart of the inquiry is a basic question of **"What wants or needs to be spoken, and why?"**

My inquiry in the current moment is somewhat different. I find myself in the midst of some personal struggle with how to get my conversational needs met. I heard myself express my "predicament" to a friend in the following way:

> *"I know that I am in search of something and my intuition tells me that there is a conversation(s) I am looking for that will meet this need. I feel a bit like Cinderella waiting for the right conversational slipper, one which will bring clarity to something inchoate in me that wants to be expressed. It's like something wanting to be born; something incipient. But I'm at a loss about what exactly I need to say or who I could say it to."*

As I heard what I said, the first thing that stood out was the theme of pregnancy and birth. The psychoanalyst in me then heard in the statement that there was something I was trying to work out in myself; something about my way of thinking/ feeling which I was trying to make sense of and organize. I also heard the articulation of very young emotional needs; the longing to be deeply seen and heard by another. In the parlance of psychoanalysis, these are "selfobject needs." There are many different selfobject needs, intertwined with every aspect of psychological development. Part of what I was expressing here seems to be the need to have my views affirmed or validated.

At one level, then, hunger for deep conversation is about a need for connection. Connection serves many relational needs. The psychological/relational need to be received, listened deeply to, and understood is very basic. We need to be deeply known by another in order to grow. In this, each of us is like a thirsty a plant which needs to be watered by the deep seeing of another.

There is a great deal that goes into this kind of deep seeing. Communication is a generative act which depends on a complex interpersonal chemistry of speaking, listening, and listening to the other's listening. There is something vital in the shared resonance we have when we "mix minds" with certain particular others. But in addition, the deepening of discourse around a particular topic often depends on the shared language we develop with others whom we come to know well. In this instance, what I wanted to talk *about* was inquiry, so I was looking for a conversation that would deepen my understanding of Buddhadharma.

In this regard, what stands out to me in my hunger for deep conversation is my experience of incipient meaning. New meanings often emerge in conversation with others, co-created in dialogue. Indeed, my thoughts are often unknown to me until I hear what comes out of my mouth. My longing was to find a relational home[19] in which my understanding could deepen and be accurately articulated. This search for meaning is closely aligned with my deep need to know.

But what I think is the most fundamental psychological level in what I was seeking has to do with what I regard as an indwelling drive for self-actualization. We strive to feel Real and to become real as ourselves; to come into being. In the words of the mystical philosopher Gurdjieff, "The world is only real when I am." At this level, the hunger for deep conversation reflects a drive for authenticity and aliveness; the need to dwell comfortably within our own skin.

As my thoughts unfolded over a period of days, and as I sat with this inquiry in meditation, I saw that what I had been thinking of as "hunger for deep conversation" had many more layers than I had previously realized. A new understanding dawned on me: at the core of the hunger for deep conversation I was experiencing was a manifestation of the desire to be; the basic hunger for existence.[20] With the recognition of this deeper meaning, the experience of urgency that had impelled the writing of this Newsletter dissolved; for now, at least, the inquiry felt complete and resolved.

26

On The Felt Sense of Emergent Meaning

"Reality lies at the frontier between what you think

is you and what you think is not you."

— David Whyte

Preamble/Context

A friend recently gifted me with a 2023 book written by psycho-therapist and meditation teacher Gary Sherman: ***Tales From A Committed Visitor: Living and Learning As Spirit In Form***. Inner Harmonics Press, Sebastopol, California.[26] The book stirred strong waves of interest and excitement within me and generated an unusually strong impulse to write about my experience of reading the book. Adding to the impact, my writing creatively unfolded in a way which itself surprised me. It took shape as a kind of open-letter to the book's author (whom I have never met). The letter follows next.

* * * * * *

Dear Gary Sherman,

Your recent book *Tales From A Committed Visitor* struck a deep chord in me. The resonance I felt was so strong that I read through the book a second time to take notes.

Apart from being amused at seeing myself in student mode, what felt very important in my reading of your book was the felt sense that your words evoked in me. As I searched for language which might convey this felt sense, punctuation seemed the best way to express what I was feeling: " !! " . There was a sense of great interest and excitement. In moments my skin tingled with goosebumps. Maybe I could say it this way: " !! " expresses the felt sense of new meaning emerging from someplace deep within me.

* * * * * *

Perhaps I should acknowledge here that " !! " is a familiar subjective experience for me. I think generally it reflects a feeling that I am in proximity to something which is both True and important (somewhere in the neighborhood of epiphany). In " !! " I sometimes feel that I now Know something more deeply than ever before; or, I have the sense of discovering something previously unknown.

As you describe in your book, there can be **transformative**

power in the recognition of new meanings. The one idea in *Tales From A Committed Visitor* that had the most important meaning for me — the strongest experience of " **!!** " — was the following:

> *"The inside of you waits to be explored. It is open and accessible to direct perception. This is where you will find what you were looking for, the completion of the self you know."*

This, I now recognize, has always been the core quest at the heart of my spiritual practice.

* * * * * * *

In your book, you describe how the lived world of experience is created from constituent elements: bodily sensations, words, pictures, and attention. You also describe at length a process which you call the "**everyday magic of speaking.**" "Speaking into being" is a wonderfully descriptive phrase: in short, it expresses the idea that language is integrally involved in manifestation.

The language we use gives meaning and coherence to our experiences, thereby influencing our perception of reality and the possibilities within it.

For me, there is everyday magic in your book. Most salient is the impact I feel in naming the *longing to connect with deeper layers of myself* and the *longing for completion*. In addition, *Tales From A Committed Visitor* reminds me of my lifelong quest to discover the *"multidimensional nature of reality"* which you so vividly described in your book. " **!!** "expresses the power of these longings.

Writing these words, it now dawns on me that the deeply embodied felt sense of " **!!** "is itself a connection to those deeper layers of myself that I long for — a small instance, perhaps, of everyday magic in action!

For whatever reason, the way you articulate your own authentically felt Truth resonates deeply within me. " !! " is, perhaps, my felt sense of an emergent integration among many layers of myself; the coming into being of a new and deepening level self-knowledge.

* * * * * * *

As I have contemplated my experience of reading *Tales From A Committed Visitor* and its impact on me, I am also struck by your description of the process you call "**inspiration**", which for you manifests as the presence of an unfamiliar voice within yourself: Quoting here from your book:

> *"I became aware of receiving knowledge and wisdom within myself. I received inspirational thought directly into my mind without any prior cognition and into my body without any physical sensory stimulus ...These were the portals through which I first became aware of the presence of the unfamiliar voice."*

> ....

> *"I started naming for myself where in my self-experience the inspiration would appear. The unfamiliar inner voice announced itself with "a feeling that appeared out of nowhere. I would have a thought that inspired a new feeling, or a feeling that generated a new thought."*

The process you call inspiration is one that I too experience — indeed, am experiencing *now*—but rather than appearing as an unfamiliar voice in my mind, it tends to come to me in conversation with others or in writing, when many times I find myself articulating ideas which previously I had not known that I thought. You designate such experiences as "**self-expressed inspiration**". I think of them as **channeling wisdom**. Not infrequently, the emergence of channeled wisdom announces itself with a felt sense of " **!!** ". Having read *Tales From A Committed Visitor*, I now recognize that in such moments I may actually be opening to the deeper portal that you call **"multidimensional inspiration."**

As you suggest in your book, we prime the conscious mind to receive inspiration by recognizing it, welcoming it, desiring it, and granting it validity through the meaning we assign to it. As I am thinking of it now, " **!!** " is an embodied experience of my intention to open myself to deeper levels of multidimensional inspiration.

* * * * * *

Pausing in the process of writing this piece, I take what in Zen might be called a "backward step" in order to see more clearly what else wants to be said.

What strikes me is that, in my experience, channeling wisdom is often paired with experiences of **synchronicity**, another portal into multidimensional inspiration. From this angle of view, it feels significant to me that your book arrived into my reality at the moment that it did, as it seems woven seamlessly together with other current events in my inner life. From a multidimensional view, messages arrive when we most need to hear them, and in hindsight, it does appear to me that *Tales From A Committed Visitor* has provided exactly the frame I need for an emergent new view of reality and my place within it.

27

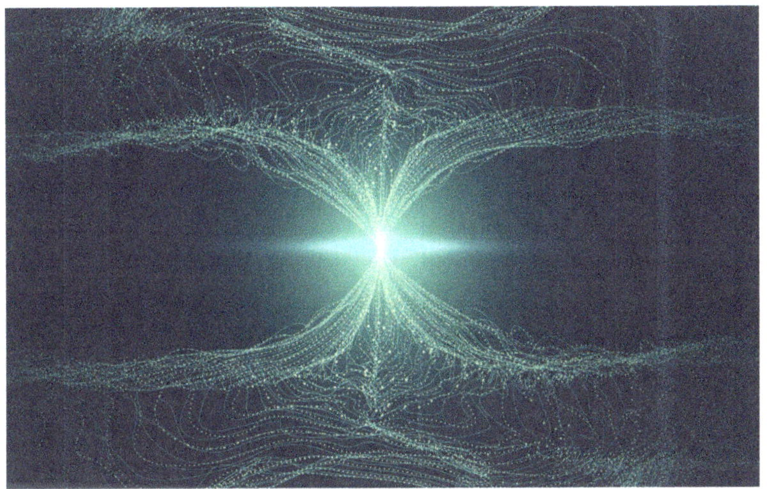

Inquiring Deeply About Transformative Conversation

Since I wrote the essay *The Hunger For Deep Conversation* (Ch. 25), I have been paying close attention to which conversations feel "deep" to me, and why. What I found was that depth has several different dimensions. For example, sometimes "deep" connoted a conversation in which I felt safe to be very open and self-revealing; a conversation which felt intensely personal. At other times, "deep" referred to the emotional resonance I felt with the other. But the kind of "deep" I am writing about here—the kind of "deep" that I am most hungry for—is deep in the sense of wise or profound, philosophical. To distinguish this dimension of depth from the others, I have decided to use the term **"transformative conversation."**

I have spent my life seeking out such conversations and have been fortunate to find friends with whom to have them. In the end, I have come to see that, for me, transformative conversation is a kind of wisdom practice; a relational form of deep inquiry.

The Relational field [21]

A good place to begin a discussion of transformative conversation is with the concept of the **relational field**: the invisible yet palpable field of energy that connects us when we are present with someone.

Depth reflects mutual Presence in the relational field: the quality of focused, receptive attention we bring to the present moment. When we slow down and attune to each other in conversation— coming into presence with one another— our mutual presence creates a synergy which amplifies our experience of depth in the relational field. Through this interpenetrating interpersonal resonance, depth of awareness can be a shared experience.

Depth also reflects the interpersonal chemistry involved in our connections with others. Such chemistry may be a function of human neurobiology: whenever we engage intently in seeing and listening to another—eye contact is important in this—there is an inter-brain synchronization that occurs, aligning our somatic and affective states [22]. In this way, we nonverbally perceive, communicate, and mutually regulate each other's subjective states. Through this interpenetrating interpersonal resonance, depth of awareness can be shared.

Deep awareness is the foundation of transformative conversation.

Deep Listening

The relational field we experience in any conversational context is a function of the field of our mutual listening. Similar to meditative listening, the heart of such listening is receptive attention to whatever is arising. It is enhanced by paying attention to the deep silence which can be found in the subjective background as we interact, sustaining attention to what is emergent.

In addition to this nonverbal awareness, how we listen to the content of what is spoken also plays a key role in experiencing depth. Meaning is expressed both in the music and in the words of what is said.

Actually, deep listening involves paying attention both to what is spoken and to what is <u>not</u> spoken. We listen to the listening of the other, and we also listen within for our felt sense of the conversational moment.[23]

What I want to emphasize here is that the symbolic meanings conveyed in language are not separate from the entire field of reactivity in the minds of both speaker and listener. We shape the relational field with our state of mind as well as with the thoughts, imagery, and feelings we bring to the conversation. Each of us has our own language, our own idiom. Meanings are *created* with the word pictures we paint in the relational field of conversation.

Deep listening is the backbone of transformative conversation.

Deep Understanding

Transformative conversation often involves the *enactment of self-reflection.* In speaking our thoughts out loud— held in the deep listening of the other— we can discover what we may not have known we thought; what has been "pre-reflectively unconscious". And— in feeling deeply seen and heard, deeply received and understood— we can expand upon our self-understanding.

This is not meant to suggest that deep conversation consists of fully formulated thoughts simply waiting to be discovered or elucidated. Rather, it often has to do with **unformulated experience**: experience not yet put into words. New meanings emerge at this boundary between what is unformulated and what is formulated; between what is unknown and what is becoming known. If we pay close attention, we may even be able to find the "felt sense" of emergent meaning—some kind of "intriguing confusion", or perhaps struggle, which we are wanting to make sense of.

Intellectual though this description may sound, the articulation of meaning in deep conversation is not primarily a conceptual process. Rather, it is comprehension grounded in intuition and empathy. Deep understanding is a process of feeling our way toward whatever meaning is unfolding. In the shared field of deep listening and understanding, the mind is enabled to tap into deep layers of the psyche and the knowledge that the unconscious holds.

Deep understanding is a relational act.

Transformative Conversation: Inquiring Deeply in the Relational Field

Many transformative conversations happen with no explicit intention or agenda beyond the desire to connect and talk, to "mix minds" with someone simply for the pleasure of it. Such conversations simply follow the thread of ideas which present themselves to be spoken. This may be likened to rowing a boat down a river, where the current of our deep mutual listening carries the conversation effortlessly along.

But, at least for me, there is another kind of transformative conversation: one which is pre-meditated, undertaken with the purpose of deepening my understanding of something. I most often seek out such conversations when I am deeply engaged in inquiring deeply about something. For example, in recent weeks I have had several conversations with others about the subjective experience of Depth. Such conversations are deliberate, if not strategic; undertaken with the intention to resolve a question or simply to create space to discover meanings which are incubating within.

I also seek out transformative 1 conversations when I want to explore something which is at the leading edge of what is unfolding in my life. In the conversational mirror of the other, it is often possible to see our struggles and difficulties more clearly. It has been my experience that there is always wisdom available when we turn *toward* rather than *away from* what we are resisting or where we are "stuck", and transformative conversations allow us to deeply encounter these places within ourselves.

What crops up in our lives is neither incidental nor accidental; it is the substance we think with and the forward face of what we will become.[24]

In short, transformative conversation provides a space in which we may be able to gain **relational freedom**[25]: the freedom to think new thoughts and to see ourselves in new ways. Transformative conversation is, I think, in service of the experience of depth itself.

Endnotes

1   Schuman, M. (2017) Mindfulness-informed Relational
    Psychotherapy and Psychoanalysis: Inquiring Deeply.
    Routledge Press, New York.

2   Kramer, G. (2007) *Insight Dialogue: The Interpersonal Path
    To Freedom*. Shambhala Press, Boston.

3   Phrase "relational home" taken from the work of
    psychoanalyst Robert Stolorow.

4   Phrase "are you willing to be changed by change?" taken from
    work of dharma teacher Phillip Moffitt.

5   Wheelis, A. (1975) *How People Change*, Harper Colophon
    Books, New York.

6   Stevens, Barry (2005) *Don't Push The River: It Flows By
    Itself*. Gestalt Journal Press. *www.Gestalt.org*

7   This is a cornerstone of the teachings of Vipassana master
    Ajahn Sumedho. Sumedho, A. (2007) *The Sound of Silence*.
    Wisdom Publications, Boston, MA.

8   Rubin, T.I. (1998) *Compassion and Self-Hate*. Touchtone
    Press, New York.

9   Auel, J.M. (1981) *Clan of The Cave Bear*. Bantam Books, New
    York.

10   Bass, A. (2001) It Takes One to Know One; or, Whose Unconscious Is It Anyway?, *Psychoanalytic Dialogues*, 11(5).

11   Relational dynamics are discussed at length in Schuman, M. (2017) *Mindfulness-Informed Relational Psychotherapy and Psychoanalysis: Inquiring Deeply*, Routledge Press, New York.

12   A newer version of this acronym uses the directives to "Recognize, Allow, Investigate, and Nurture".

13   Schuman (2018) Speaking and Listening: The Intimate Dance of Speaking and Communicating. *Wise Brain Bulletin*, 12(5).

14   Redding, K. (2022) *Ten Ways to Awaken the Wise Heart: A Photographic Journey*. Creative Press, Anaheim CA.

15   Shafer, R. (1992) *Retelling A Life: Narration and Dialogue in Psychoanalysis*. Basic Books, New York.

16   Title of film which documents Erhard Seminars Training (Werner Erhard, 1978).

17   Schuman, M. (2019). Inquiring Deeply About Equanimity. *Wise Brain Bulletin*, 3(5): 16–25.

18   For example, see Schuman (2006) *Driven To Distraction: Observations on Obsessionality*. in Cooper, P. (ed) Into the Mountain Stream: Psychoanalysis and Buddhist Experience. Rowman & Littlefield, Maryland.

19   Term borrowed from the work of Robert Stolorow.

20 In Buddhism what is called *bhava-taṇhā*, the basic hunger for existence.

21 The relational field is explored in my book, Schuman, M. (2017) *"Mindfulness-Informed Relational Psychotherapy and Psychoanalysis: Inquiring Deeply"*. Routledge Press, New York.

22 See for example Schore, A.N. (2021) *Front. Psychol.* Vol. 12

23 In early psychoanalysis, this quality of attention was called "listening with the third ear" [Reik,T. (1949) *Listening With The Third Ear*. Farrar, Strauss & Co. New York]

24 Hirschfield, J. (1998) *Nine Gates: Entering The Mind of Poetry*. Harper Perennial, New York.

25 Stern, Donnel (2017) *Relational Freedom*. Routledge Press, New York.

26 Sherman, G. (2023) *Tales From A Committed Visitor: Living and Learning As Spirit In Form*. Inner Harmonics Press, Sebastopol, California.

PHOTO CREDITS

Page 45, Edward Munch, *"The Scream"*.

Page 105, photo by Drew Dizzy Graham, from Unsplash.

All other photos licensed by Shutterstock.

About The Author

Marjorie Schuman, Ph.D. is a clinical psychologist whose career has focused on the integration of mindful awareness and psychodynamic psychotherapy. In addition to her training in psychoanalysis, Marjorie has had four decades of experience practicing Buddhist insight meditation in the Theravadan tradition. She is the author of Mindfulness-Informed Relational Psychotherapy and Psychoanalysis: Inquiring Deeply (Routledge Press, 2017), and writes Inquiring Deeply Newsletter which provides probing commentary on meditation and psychotherapy: https://www.drmarjorieschuman.com Marjorie teaches and practices psychotherapy in Santa Barbara, CA.